BROKEN
SILENCE
A Secret Life of Abuse

By Dr. Nesa Chappelle

EDITING
On Demand
Any subject. Any style. Any time.

www.editingondemand.com

Editors:
Elaine W. Smith
Miriam W. Tarver
Ruth Thaler-Carter
Regina Williams

Dog Ear Publishing
4010 West 86th Street
Suite H
Indianapolis, IN 46268
www.dogearpublishing.net

Broken Silence: A Secret Life of Abuse is a memoir by Dr. Nesa Chappelle. Places, events, and situations are as accurate an account as could be recalled by the author. Some names have been changed.

First published by Dog Ear Publishing

ISBN: 978-145750-656-7

Printed in the United States of America

Acknowledgments

To: E.D. Arrington, who encouraged me to write this book for my own healing; Randy Griffin, my son, who continuously and lovingly encouraged me to forge forward with my divine assignment even when I felt the struggle was unbearable; Miss Randi, my beautiful granddaughter, for her unconditional love and her unknowing motivation; Jennie Gilliam-Hooker, my lifelong friend and confidante, who helped me to remember the pieces that make up this book; Kris Chinn, who has been with me since the fourth grade and always pushed me to be all that I could be; Elaine Watkins Smith, for her loving guidance and direction on the final preparation of this book; Dr. Michael Frazier, for steadfastly refusing to allow me to give up on my dream of receiving a Ph.D.; Dr. Julia Jordan-Zachery, for her unwavering support and belief in my ability to finish what I started; Faye Northcutt, who kept me grounded as I weathered my storms; Phil McLaurin, for trusting that I would get the job done against all the odds; Hazel Logan, who gave me her ear without judgment whenever I needed to vent; and last but not least, my father, who instilled in me the importance of education, and is responsible for my drive to be all that I can be.

A Note from the Author

Before reading the details of my journey, allow me to share with you what I expressed as a keynote speaker to the U.S. Parole Commission (USPC) in 2008 at the first conference of its Victim/Witness Program. The audience was composed primarily of commission staff, commissioners, and law enforcement and correctional officers — all devoted to assisting abused and battered men, women and children. As a survivor of domestic violence, I gave careful thought as to how I saw the Commission's role. I stated in my speech that the Commission's role was simply to "save lives."

My prayer for those who are in abusive relationships is to seek help immediately and remove yourselves and your children from an unsafe, violent, and ungodly environment.

According to the National Domestic Abuse Hotline, you may be in an abusive relationship if your spouse or partner:

- Embarrasses you with "put-downs"
- Looks at you or acts in ways that scare you
- Controls what you do, who you see or talk to, or where you go
- Stops you from seeing your friends or family members
- Takes your money or Social Security check, makes you ask for money, or refuses to give you money
- Makes all of the decisions
- Tells you that you're a bad parent or threatens to take away or hurt your children
- Prevents you from working or attending school
- Acts like the abuse is no big deal, it's your fault, or even denies doing it

- Destroys your property or threatens to kill your pets
- Intimidates you with guns, knives or other weapons
- Shoves you, slaps you, chokes you, or hits you
- Forces you to drop charges
- Threatens to commit suicide, or
- Threatens to kill you

The National Abuse Hotline Number is 1-800-799-7233 (SAFE) or 1-800-799-7234.

You are worthy of love that does not hurt and a life free from abuse.

Nesa Chappelle, Ph.D.

PROLOGUE

His verbal assault began earlier that evening…an unprovoked assault…the last assault that I would endure from him, and it was an ugly encounter. Angry as usual, always angry about something. There was always some kind of drama involving or initiated by Franklin. I can't remember every detail, but I do remember that Franklin was standing in the dining area and I was standing at the edge of the family room. Out of nowhere, he began to rehash my relationship with a former boyfriend, Solomon Hughes. Franklin shouted, clasping a bottle of beer in his hand, "He was nothing but a big, fat, stupid mother-fucker!" And those were the kindest words about Solomon that came out of his mouth. Franklin continued degrading Solomon, belittling him, making fun of my former friend — someone who he did not know and never met. His ranting and raving was not unusual. In fact, his attacks on me concerning Solomon had become a common occurrence. You see, it wasn't Solomon my husband was directing his anger at — not really. It was me he was gunning for. Whenever he thought it was time for me to get my verbal, mental, and emotional whipping, time for him to show me who was in control, Franklin picked a fight. And he was never satis-fied until he had let loose his rage on me like an unrelenting tidal wave. But on this particular day, I'd had enough. Regardless of what he said, I did not say a word. I grabbed the keys to my SUV, calmly left the family room, walked out of the door leading to the garage, and climbed into my GMC Envoy parked in the driveway. As I started the engine, I realized I didn't get my glasses or my purse. That was one time I didn't care about what I did not have; it was time to go.

Franklin followed me out and positioned himself boldly in front of my truck, his demeanor and demonic eyes daring me to as much as budge. I studied him through the front windshield. I was left with two choices — drive forward and run him over, or put the car in reverse and back up across my beautifully landscaped lawn and get the hell out of harm's way. Here is where I decided that he was not worth my going to jail, so I put the pedal to the metal and hurriedly backed the SUV across the lawn onto the roadway behind our beautiful home.

* * *

I was now fully conscious of the fact that I was not in just another abusive relationship. I was not just married to a man with characteristics or traits similar to those of my former abusive husbands, but I was also married to a man who was like my father. So I wondered, how could such a well-educated, gainfully employed, independent woman, who had taken good care of her physical self, end up in another abusive relationship?

CHAPTER 1
MY FAMILY

As a young child, I craved my mother's love — to feel it, to experience her warmth — and this became the one constant desire in my life. As an adolescent, I dreamed of a strong, healthy, happy mother-daughter relationship. I wasn't sure what such a relationship felt like, but I instinctively knew that I wanted it. In addition to needing to feel my mother's love, I longed for the day I would live with her and we would be best friends. She would teach me about life. We would laugh and cry together. I would listen to her tell me interesting, colorful stories about her life and loves in the rural South in the mid-1940s. We would travel and shop together as well as confide untold secrets to each other. She would boast about my accomplishments to family and friends.

To complete my dream, I wanted to someday marry a good man who adored me. My husband would be the man I loved deeply — a partner to share my life with, the man I would grow old with. Given my young optimism, the day would certainly come when I would be blessed with a kind husband to care and provide for me. He would be my protector. I envisioned that we would live in a lovely home, vacation in beautiful places abroad, and enjoy a life filled with excitement and adventure. At the time, dreams were all I had — they certainly were not a reality — but they allowed me to be optimistic and look forward to the day when these fantasies would become reality. As I moved toward adulthood, my dreams became more difficult to envision as reality, given the turbulent and uncertain world into which I was born. At times, it felt as if I were on a bumpy, nausea-producing, never-ending roller coaster ride called life — my life.

I was born in 1951 in Washington, DC, at Freedmen's Hospital to Bethezel Chappelle and Never Duncan, Jr. My mother and father never married and always lived apart. I was told that during my mother's pregnancy, my father, who suffered with allergies and asthma, was not sure that I was his child. After my birth, when he was allowed to see me through the hospital window, I sneezed. He laughed and said, "Yeah, that's mine."

My father had no desire, or maybe believed he had no reason, to commit himself to any one woman. Handsome and sexy, he wanted the best of everything his money could afford. He wore fine suits, dined in high-class restaurants, drove fancy eye-catching cars, and carried large sums of money. Confident and smart, his demeanor demanded respect, and he was the type of man who easily attracted women. Because he could be with almost any woman he fancied with little or no effort, Daddy changed women as often as he changed his shoes. As a young man, his mother reluctantly sent him to live in Washington, DC. Rumor had it that she wanted him far away from southern white women who, she said, "worried him to death." During the early 1930s, a Negro living in the South would surely be lynched for merely glancing at a white woman and this terrified her.

My father had very light skin and if not for the texture of his hair, he could have easily passed for white. He proudly claimed his African American heritage while at the same time bragging about how people would comment that he "looked white." My father marveled at his light skin color, but I didn't understand the significance of light skin or its significance in the black community until adulthood. People told me that I was his spitting image. An interesting man, he had more than good looks. He was extremely intelligent and had the "gift of gab," which he needed for his hustle. Daddy was brilliant, articulate, and politically astute, frequently reminding me and anyone else that if he had been afforded the opportunity to get further than sixth grade, he could have been a university president. He always admired and respected educated blacks.

At 32, my father decided to circumvent the barriers that kept Negroes poor, and became a hustler — a numbers backer and gambler. He genuinely believed hustling was the only way that he, an uneducated Negro man from the South, could financially succeed and achieve the American Dream, a dream that at the time did not include Negroes who were struggling to win the right to vote without intimidation and violence.

Daddy wanted me to have an easier life, and, given his lifestyle, did the best he could to ensure it. As far back as I can remember, he routinely stopped by to leave money for my care. Money meant everything to him because in his mind it secured his independence and afforded him a comfortable life. It allowed him to be in a position where his "manhood" could not be compromised, and more importantly, he would not be forced to bow down to and rely on any white man for survival. He also believed that by providing money for my care, his parental obligations were fulfilled. To his credit, he spent many Sunday afternoons with me. If we did not go to dinner, we visited the corner drugstore and sat at the counter to have my favorite cone of chocolate ice cream. My father was responsible for introducing me to what he termed "the good life," as he wanted the best for his little girl, but his lifestyle left little time for the emotional fulfillment I needed.

* * *

One summer when I was four years old, Daddy drove me to his hometown of Woodruff, South Carolina, to meet his parents, Mamie and Never Duncan, Sr. I loved them both immediately. They were warm, loving, and nurturing. I remember crying buckets when it was time to return home. I didn't want to leave my newfound family, including cousins my age. By age seven, I had traveled alone on a train to South Carolina to visit my grandparents. Grandpa Neb did not have a car so he would hire a driver to bring him to the train station to meet me. There, he would wait for my arrival, always wearing overalls and a wide straw hat. The second he laid eyes on me, he would yelp at the top of his lungs, "Yonder come my sweet sang!" Oh, how I relished his welcomes. In those precious moments, I felt special, like I was somebody important, that I mattered. During the thirty-minute ride to my grandparents' small country-frame house, I was filled with anticipation of seeing Grandma

Mamie, my cousins, and my friends. As soon as the driver parked the car under the big pecan tree in their yard, Grandma would come bouncing out the back door of the house and down the steps to greet me. I was just as eager; leaping out of the car, running to her, and throwing myself into her outstretched arms that held me ever so tightly.

Grandpa Neb was a handsome man of average build. In fact, Daddy looked exactly like him, but looks were not all that father and son had in common. They both had the highest respect for Grandma Mamie and provided as best they could for her, but of course they both loved women and the women loved them. "Neb used to love to run them women," Grandma Mamie once told me. "I used to have to go git'im and make'im come home!" But unlike my father, when I was with Grandpa Neb, he was always the same — quiet, easygoing, and loving. You never knew how to take Daddy, who was mercurial — up one minute and down the next, talking sweet one minute and screaming the next. At times he would get extremely angry, shaking his head vigorously until his blood pressure shot sky high, sending him to bed with headaches.

Grandma Mamie was a dark-brown, small-framed, feisty, God-fearing woman, with shoulder-length, straight black hair. She walked with such an air of pride that if she held her head any higher and it rained, she would have surely drowned. On Sundays, Grandma Mamie would dress Antoinette, my "twin cousin," and me for church in our "Sunday-go-to-meeting" clothes. Her friends and neighbors called us twins because we looked remarkably alike. She would parade us around, and proudly boast on me, "This here is my grandbaby from Washington, DC." My dear sweet grandparents knew how to make me feel extra special, if only for a short while. Grandpa Neb died at age seventy-seven. Twelve years after he died, Daddy moved Grandma Mamie into his apartment to take care of her. Because it was difficult to take care of her, one year later he placed her in a nursing home where she received the care she needed. Grandma died quietly in her sleep at the age of ninety-two. Now and then, when I allow my mind to wander back over our visits that I hold ever so fondly, I am thankful that Grandpa Neb and Grandma Mamie did not witness my turbulent adult life.

* * *

My Family

My mother, Bethezel Chappelle, fondly referred to as Betty or "Lil Sis," was a twin. She was born in Clinton, South Carolina, to Eunice and Conway Chappelle. She was weak, sickly, and dark-skinned, with flaming red hair. Bethuel Chappelle, known as Beth, her twin, was referred to as "Big Sis," and was the exact opposite of my mother — born healthy, with a light complexion and thick black hair. One of my aunts once told me that my mother was often teased for being dark with red hair.

Grandma Eunice and Grandpa Conway were dirt-poor and between the two of them, were the parents of fourteen children. Grandma Eunice bore four children by Grandpa Conway: Carrie; Eunice, who was named after her mother; and the twins, Bethezel and Beth. The remaining ten children were from their previous marriages, and I came to know four intimately: Aunt Constance, Uncle Gregory, Uncle Cordell, Jr., and Uncle Dennis.

During the mid-1940s, my mother left her South Carolina hometown to join her older sisters and brothers, already settled in Washington, DC. At the age of twenty-three, she got a job working at Brown's Beer Garden, a Northwest nightclub, where she met my father, who was ten years her senior. A romance ensued and I was born two years later.

I called my mother "Ma." Like my father, she did not have a clue about parenting. She was young, wild, and nowhere near ready to be tied down with a baby. I saw her as infrequently as I saw my father. My mother was considered a woman of average looks — tall, with a brick-house figure, and based on what I heard about her, had no problem getting the attention of a man. Like my father, my mother's lifestyle left little room for a child. But, unlike my father, my mother did not have parents for me to spend summers with. My mother seldom spoke to me about her parents, who died before I was born.

What little I learned about my mother's side of the family came mostly from Aunt Eunice. She was the only sister who would speak openly about their family history. She said that their mother, Eunice Chappelle, was a short, brown-skinned woman with wide hips — a family trait. Their father, Conway Chappelle, was a tall, light-skinned, handsome man with a gorgeous head of thick black hair. When I look at the picture of Grandpa Conway, I now see that my son closely resembles his great-grandfather.

Grandpa Conway died of leukemia when my mother was a young girl and Grandma Ella suffered with severe hypertension for years. Aunt Carrie, Aunt Beth, and my mother left Clinton to join their other siblings in Washington, DC, leaving Aunt Eunice behind to care for their ailing mother until her death. She then joined her brothers and sisters in Washington, DC, with her two children, Charles and Pamela.

CHAPTER 2

LIVING WITH AUNT CONSTANCE

My mother and I lived on the third floor of a rooming house on Corcoran Street, between 13th and 14th Streets NW, until I was three years old. We moved in with Aunt Constance, the oldest of the fourteen siblings, and one of her brothers, Uncle Gregory. From a child's eye, the house appeared grand. Uncle Gregory owned the spacious three-bedroom rowhouse, which was located in a middle-class black neighborhood on Meridian Place NW, a narrow street between Newton and Oak Streets. A beautiful mahogany piano, prominently placed against the wall of the lengthy hallway on the main floor, caught the attention of everyone entering the house. On the left side of the hallway was the parlor, used only to entertain special guests; at the back of the house was our family room, where everyone gathered. Behind the family room was a large kitchen overlooking a spacious fenced-in backyard.

A short walk past the piano on the left side of the hallway, before reaching the family room, was a flight of stairs that led to the basement where Uncle Cordell lived for a brief period. A staircase in the same area led to the three bedrooms on the second floor. Uncle Gregory occupied the smallest bedroom at the farthest end of the hallway near the bathroom. Aunt Constance and I shared the largest bedroom at the opposite end of the hall overlooking Meridian Place. When my mother was home, which was very seldom, she occupied the medium-sized middle bedroom.

I got to see my mother more often when we moved in with Aunt Constance, if only for very short periods of time when she would make brief appearances. I missed her and wanted to spend more time with her. Most nights, I would lie in the bed I shared with my aunt listening for the tap-tap-tap of her high-heeled shoes against the concrete sidewalk in front of the house. Whenever I heard steps close to the house, I would spring from the bed, race excitedly to the window and peer out, searching in the darkness for my mother. Other nights, I would sit by the window, gazing out, hoping to see her get out of a car, walk up the steps of the house; or I would listen for the click of her key turning the lock to the front door. On those rare occasions when my mother did come home, I stuck to her like glue as much as she would allow. She was uncomfortable expressing affection, at least to me; so to express my affection without annoying her, I would bend over and kiss her arm. I loved to kiss her arm, which totally irritated her. "Stop that," she would snap. Disappointed and hurt, I would stop, because I never wanted to make her angry, afraid that if I did, she might leave again and not come back.

But it didn't matter what I did or did not do, sooner rather than later that dreadful moment always came — she would bathe, get dressed, and leave. I would cry, scream, heave, and sob. Sometimes she would try to soothe me, telling me to stop crying, telling me that she would be right back. Those empty words did nothing to console my aching heart, because once my mother left, I had no idea how long it would be before I saw her again. There were times, to avoid a scene with me, when she would simply sneak out of the house; but other times, she ignored my tears altogether. It was as if she was devoid of emotion, unable to hear me, see me, or feel my pain. She had somewhere to go and that was that.

It bothered Aunt Constance to see me cry for my mother. She would pick me up from the floor where I would collapse in tears and take me into the bedroom we shared. Usually, Uncle Gregory and my aunt would come up with ways to console me. One sure way was for Uncle Gregory to sing "A Tisket, A Tasket," a popular song for children in my day. "A tisket, a tasket, I lost my yellow basket" — he knew how much I loved to hear him sing that song to me. I would giggle and sing along with him and we would both laugh. Uncle Gregory had a contagious laugh, and I

Living with Aunt Constance

remember it to this day. He was a quiet, easygoing man of average height and build with soft brown skin, and he was very narcissistic. Periodically, Uncle Gregory suffered from severe migraine headaches that incapacitated him for days, sometimes as long as a week. During those times I had to be very quiet. The doctors never discovered what caused those terrible headaches because neurology in those days was far from what it is today. He worked for the federal government as a security guard but could usually be found gambling away his earnings, shooting craps, at the neighborhood joint at the corner of Meridian Place and Fourteenth Street.

Uncle Gregory was smooth as fine wine. He loved to dress in expensive suits and was very much a ladies' man, a player who had an eye for young women. Mildred Moss was a lady with whom he spent considerable time. She was somewhat unattractive — tall, with dark-brown skin and protruding teeth. According to Aunt Constance, Mildred was very smart and held a high-level government job, which was rare for a Negro woman in the 1950s. Mildred and Aunt Constance attended the same church and were close friends. Mildred made no secret of her love for Uncle Gregory and regularly visited him at the house. Although he respected her intelligence and professionalism, and spent time with her, he was not in love with her, but she desperately loved him. She was his dear friend with a fringe benefit — sex — and she remained an integral part of his life until the day he died.

Uncle Cordell was six feet, three inches tall, a solidly built, dark-skinned man who loved to dance and hang out downtown with his friends. He showed up at the house mostly to bathe and change clothes. When he was a young boy, while working on a farm in South Carolina, he lost his left arm in an accident involving a tractor. When I was young, I thought Uncle Cordell was the strongest one-armed man who ever lived. He would grab the back of my dress or shirt with his teeth, lift me up with his right hand, and place me on his shoulders. I would hold onto his neck tightly while he walked with me on his shoulders from Meridian Place to 14th and T Streets to see Daddy. It always amazed me to watch how easily he tied his shoes using one hand. I adored my Uncle Cordell.

Like Uncle Gregory, Uncle Cordell had an eye for young girls, but, unlike his brother, he was jealous and physically abusive to women. In fact, I was told that after learning that his young girlfriend was cheating on him, he nearly beat her to death with his one fist. Of course, I remember seeing his trophy girlfriend a number of times; but after that incident, she disappeared. According to Aunt Constance, the young lady spent a long time in the hospital as a result of Uncle Cordell's beating.

There is no doubt that my uncles loved me because I was their niece. As a child, when you love someone unconditionally as I loved my uncles, you don't think about them being violent with their women, even when you overhear conversations about their transgressions. I did not understand domestic violence then. All I knew was that I had fun with my uncles.

Aunt Constance was light-skinned with the same attractive facial features as Grandpa Conway. Her hair color was her signature and it was rinsed a beautiful blue-gray that not many women could carry. It looked absolutely stunning on her. She was medium height and had a figure like the shape of a Coca Cola bottle — big breasts, small waist, wide hips, a voluptuous rear-end, and strong, shapely legs. My aunt was fully aware that she was "hot" and took delight in flaunting her sex appeal. She was a churchgoing woman who invited eager and willing churchgoing men to her home for a social hour or two — or three. Once I walked in on Aunt Constance having sex in the parlor with Mr. Joe, a married deacon in her church, who was one of quite a few men she entertained in the privacy of her parlor.

None of her sisters, including my mother, was fond of Aunt Constance. They accused her of stirring up confusion in the family — lying, backstabbing, and gossiping until everybody in the family was angry with each other because of some lie she started. Because my mother had so much disdain for her sister, I wondered why she allowed me to live with her instead of with Aunt Carrie, Aunt Eunice, or Aunt Beth. However, in hindsight, she was the only sister in a position to care for me. The others had more than their share of issues. All but one made poor choices in men, and they were all struggling to care for their own children.

My mother's twin sister, Aunt Beth, a strikingly beautiful, big-boned woman, married Wilbur Hall, the most gentle and pleasant man I have ever met. Uncle Wilbur was a dark-complexioned man of average height. His adorable smile showed off deep dimples in each cheek and he had a naturally kind demeanor. Uncle Wilbur was no match for his young, strong-willed, streetwise wife. He was a happy, cheerful, gentle, hard-working family man who loved Aunt Beth and their daughter, Loretta. But if Aunt Beth loved him at all, she loved her freedom and the streets more. She lived her life more fervently than my mother. A strong, free-spirited, rebellious, and independent woman, she could not get enough of the fast life, and lived life on her terms.

While still married to Uncle Wilbur, Aunt Beth set her sights on a married man, Jack Butrell, who was the first cousin of the man my mother would later marry. Jack had a smooth, dark Hershey chocolate complexion. He was handsome, outgoing, successful, and was employed as a construction supervisor for a major construction company. His nickname was "Cadillac Jack" because he purchased a new Cadillac every two years. The times that I saw Aunt Beth and Jack together, it was clear that she loved that man. Of course, her love for him did not prevent the mountain of problems they encountered. Even though he was married, Jack was jealous and controlling, but Aunt Beth could not and would not be controlled. Nobody, including Jack, was going to dictate her life, so she would not back away from physical encounters. She was known to beat down an average man and would not hesitate to take on anybody who challenged her. Because of the contentious nature of their relationship, Aunt Beth and Cadillac Jack often fought toe-to-toe like two men. To this day, Loretta is a nervous wreck because of her mother's ongoing verbal and physical altercations with Cadillac Jack. Then there were the other problems — major problems.

Aunt Beth, to my knowledge, never divorced Uncle Wilbur, but staked claim on Jack even though he was married. Actually, they staked claim on each other. The biggest problem was that Jack had no intention of leaving his wife, Anne, who was a plain, brown-skinned woman with a model figure even after giving birth to his five children. There were times when Anne would call Aunt Beth's apartment to speak with her husband,

and depending on my aunt's mood, she would allow it or she would curse Anne out as if she was the offended spouse. Jack's wife had an ace card up her sleeve that she played often and it was always a winning move. She and Jack had one daughter, Chante, who was disabled. Jack cherished her like none of his other children. Whenever his wife called to ask him to come home because Chante was sick, he would drop Aunt Beth like a hot potato and rush off to see about his precious daughter. Nevertheless, my aunt maintained a turbulent relationship with him for more than twenty years. It ended when she died of cancer at the age of fifty-four.

Aunt Eunice was a medium-brown-skinned woman with large hips, medium waist, and small legs. She more closely resembled her mother and was known as the sister the others could count on during a season of illness. Aunt Eunice was hilarious, and after a few cocktails, became loud and boisterous. She would — as they said back in the day — "tell it like it is, taking no prisoners." She could out-curse any sailor, and would twist every story told to her so out of context that it was news to the originator. Simply put, if you wanted the entire family to know about something, tell Aunt Eunice. She got information out to the family faster than the Postal Service, but it was always distorted.

Aunt Eunice met and married Charles Simpson, Sr., while living in South Carolina, where they had two children, Charles, Jr., and Pamela. In DC, she met and married J.W. Watson — a light-skinned man with wavy black hair — and they had one child, Sharon. If you did not know Uncle J.W., you would easily believe that he was the most outgoing, friendliest person you ever met. However, nothing was further from the truth. The real Uncle J.W. was a lazy drunk who physically and emotionally abused his wife and children. He treated Charles, Jr., his stepson, so badly that the boy was forced to leave home to live with Aunt Beth and Loretta. To this day, the abuse that Charles Jr. experienced with J.W. still haunts him. Aunt Eunice left Uncle J.W. several times but always returned to him before finally garnering the will, courage, and strength to leave him for good. Aunt Eunice's leaving surely did not break Uncle J.W.'s heart, because shortly after their separation, he married Leah, a woman who lived a few houses down from the home he once shared with Aunt Eunice. I can only surmise that Aunt Eunice loved Uncle J.W. more than anyone knew, because when she learned of his marriage to Leah, it cut her to the core. Her marriage to J.W. Whittle proved to be a traumatic experience that she carried to her grave.

Aunt Carrie was the heaviest of the four sisters, with huge breasts, a large rear-end, and thick legs. She had a medium light-brown complexion and wore a wig most of her life to cover her naturally thin, short hair. Everyone in the family understood that Aunt Carrie was not a rocket scientist; however, she had a good heart and always strived to avoid conflict, and acted as a mediator for the family. She loved all of her sisters and worked hard to keep peace among them, although her favorite sister was Aunt Eunice. Aunt Carrie married Wesley Shepherd, Sr. (Uncle Shep), a big, robust, tall, dark-skinned man, who drove a cab and owned a gas station on Benning Road NE. He was an excellent provider for his family; Aunt Carrie never had to work outside of the home, and her sisters always said that she was lucky to have married him. She and Uncle Shep had four children — Diane, Wesley, Margaret Ann, and Malcolm. Their family was permanently disrupted when she abruptly left Uncle Shep for another man. I believed Uncle Shep was a gentle giant, but it was rumored that Aunt Carrie left him because, at times, he was abusive to her. Another rumor was that Aunt Carrie had an insatiable sexual appetite, and, thus, began to have extramarital affairs. Whatever the truth, her four children never forgave her for abandoning the family.

To my mother's credit, of the sisters and uncles I have mentioned thus far, she left me in the care of the most stable person. Her half-sister, Aunt Constance, who was unmarried, worked every day as a domestic, and had no children — a void I suspect she expected me to fill.

Aunt Constance's dream was for me to become a great pianist. She always said, "Nesa, you can always make money and have a decent life if you know how to play the piano." She was determined that I would never work as a domestic like she did. Because of her lack of education, she worked for many years as a maid for rich white folks.

Every Saturday morning without fail, Aunt Constance took me by bus across town to a music school on Georgia Avenue to study piano. One particular Saturday, she took me to music class and my mother was supposed to pick me up. When the class ended, my mother had not arrived, so there I sat in the waiting room for what seemed like hours when all of a sudden Aunt Constance burst into the room. She was visibly upset that my mother neglected to pick me up, furious that I had been forgotten. When we arrived home, she prepared lunch for me and muttered something about what would happen to me if she was not around.

Despite my efforts to be proficient at playing the piano, I only learned to play a poor rendition of "Old MacDonald." I wish that I had enjoyed learning to play the piano, but it did not interest me in the least. I was not about to tell my aunt, but she found out anyway that I hated piano lessons from my best friend's mother, Marge Brinkley. Aunt Constance and Mrs. Brinkley were talking in the foyer one day when, out of the blue, Mrs. Brinkley mentioned that I told her that I did not like playing the piano. Aunt Constance twisted her full-figured body around to me, raised her strong hand, and slapped my face. I was stunned!

Although she told too many lies, and kept confusion stirred up in the family, my aunt provided me with a clean and safe place to live, gave me wholesome food to eat, took me to church with her every Sunday, and sent me to school every day. Like my father, education was also on the top of her list for me and she repeatedly stressed that I could make something of myself and could be anything I wanted to be.

Occasionally, Aunt Constance and I went on fun outings — the beach, the park, the pool, church picnics, and other church outings. On Sundays, we always had our family dinner, where my aunt, Uncle Gregory, sometimes Uncle Cordell, and I would sit at the kitchen table and eat a delicious southern home-cooked meal together. Sunday was the day we ate together as a family — my aunt and uncles. It was a ritual not to be broken.

Another memorable moment with my aunt occurred in 1963 when I was twelve years old. She took me to the Lincoln Memorial to hear Dr. Martin Luther King, Jr. deliver his "I Have a Dream" speech. We spread a blanket on the lawn and sat there for hours waiting for Dr. King to speak. Everyone was excited and anxiously waiting to hear this famous

Negro preacher from Atlanta, Georgia, talk about justice and freedom for colored people. The atmosphere was magical, and that moment can only be compared to time spent with my Grandpa Neb and Grandma Mamie.

Still, I did not stop missing my mother. I was desperate to be with her. I ached to be with her, even though she did not have a clue, nor did she seem to care. Maybe it was because my mother believed I was secure and well-cared-for by my aunt. Perhaps she believed there was no need for her to worry about me.

CHAPTER 3
A NEW FAMILY

In 1960, my mother left Aunt Constance's home and married Theodore Booth, a six-foot-tall, medium-brown-skinned, pigeon-toed man with a thick black moustache. Everyone called him "Teddy." I was ten years old when, a couple of months into their marriage, my mother fell victim to a serious heart ailment. Doctors discovered a mass dangerously close to her heart, which required extensive surgery. The surgeon literally cut my mother in half, leaving a scar that ran from under her left breast around her back and ended beneath her right shoulder blade. The illness, coupled with the operation, took a toll on her shapely body. No one in the family believed that she would survive, but she beat the odds. It was a miracle. After a lengthy confinement, she was released from the hospital and went to recuperate at Aunt Constance's house because she needed daily care — not because she wanted to be there. We were temporarily living under the same roof again.

Teddy remained at their apartment while my mother recuperated, but visited her every day after work. I couldn't wait to get home from school to check on her. She was extremely weak and fragile and needed my assistance. I was happy to help whenever I could. One day I came home from school and she was gone — she had returned to her apartment. Years later, I learned from my mother in one of our rare conversations that Aunt Constance had treated her horribly during her illness. The already strained relationship between my mother and her oldest sister worsened during her recuperation at my aunt's house. And, of course, my Aunt Constance continued to telephone family members to gossip and stir up trouble concerning my mother.

My mother continued to heal from the surgery. Then, what I thought was another miracle happened. My mother was thirty-six years old and pregnant. She was ecstatic, and I was excited that I was going to have a little brother or sister. I began to spend most weekends at my mother's and stepfather's apartment, which gave me an opportunity to persuade her to let me come to live with her. At first, she didn't say yes or no. Life went on as usual, but I didn't give up. Whenever I was near my mother and had the slightest opportunity, I asked to live with her. "Ma, I want to come live with you. Please." My begging was met with "We'll see," or that dreaded silence.

Because my mother was still fragile from her surgery, she worried profusely during her pregnancy that she might not be able to carry the baby to full term. Again she beat the odds, and on December 26, 1962, seven months into a very difficult pregnancy, she gave birth to Theodore Booth, Jr. He was a beautiful, brown butterball baby. I fell in love with him at first sight and pitched right in doing whatever an eleven-year-old girl could do to help care for her baby brother.

Unmistakably proud parents, I witnessed how my mother and Teddy smothered their baby boy with a deep love, devotion, and undivided attention. It was every bit the picture of a happy family, similar to TV's "Father Knows Best" or "Leave it to Beaver." Only this time I played a role in it, but fantasy is all it was. Like any fantasy, in a matter of time, reality eventually sets in.

Before the baby was born, I had almost given up hope of ever waking up under the same roof with my mother. But to my surprise, one weekend while visiting with her, she finally said that I could live with her. The day I dreamed about had finally arrived; I was going to live with my mother, and was happy and excited. When Aunt Constance learned that my mother was taking me to live with her, she was crushed and angry. She carried on with my mother as if her heart had been torn apart. She turned to me and said, "I'm the only real mother you have." She was unable or unwilling to understand why I wanted to leave the security of her home to be with a woman who barely saw or even knew me, or even pretended that she wanted me. Although Aunt Constance may not have known how I felt about her, I sincerely cared about her and appreciated the good life that she provided for me. I did not intentionally plan to hurt her by leaving to be with my mother, but I am afraid I may have done just that.

I was twelve years old when Aunt Constance had all of my clothes packed, and my mother and stepfather picked me up from her house on a Friday evening. As my stepfather loaded the bags in the trunk of his car, I jumped in the back seat, eagerly looking forward to being with my mother permanently. On the short ride to my new home, I didn't once think about Aunt Constance. I thought about my new school, Ruth K. Webb, and what it would be like. It was newly built with state-of-the-art equipment and modern classrooms. The previous schools I attended had been old and rundown. Everything in Webb was clean, bright, and organized, just as I imagined my life would be at my new home with my mother and stepfather. When we arrived at their duplex apartment, I dashed up the steps into the living room that would also serve as my bedroom. It did not matter to me that I would have to sleep on a pull-out sofa bed instead of the big bed that I shared with my aunt. In that moment, the only important thing to me was that I was with my mother. I would eat, sleep, and breathe the same air and live under the same roof with her. My dream had come true. But it gradually turned into a nightmare.

It was not long before frequent fights began to erupt between Ma and Teddy. I remember vividly one evening when an insurance agent came to the apartment to discuss life insurance coverage with my mother and stepfather. Upon completing a review of the various types of policies available, the agent waited for them to decide which policy they wanted to buy. My stepfather told my mother which policy he thought was best for the family, but she made the mistake of disagreeing with him in front of the insurance agent. Incensed, my stepfather was able to restrain himself long enough for the agent to leave the apartment, but immediately after he left, a heated argument ensued. My mother held her ground about the policy she believed was best, and Teddy unleashed his anger by hitting her. The two began to physically fight. I was not accustomed to violence at all; it was the first time I had ever seen a fight. I screamed and yelled hysterically for them to stop, but the fighting ended only when they were both too exhausted to continue. After their violent clash, my mother realized that her front teeth (a partial plate) were missing. Upset, she asked if I had seen them. I had not, but helped her to search for them. After the fight, Teddy went to sleep on the sofa. As I walked past the sofa, I noticed through my peripheral vision something clinging to his hair on the top of his head. I crept over to him and lo and behold, lodged in his hair were my mother's front teeth. That was clear evidence of her intention to bite the living hell out of Teddy. I cautiously plucked the teeth from his hair and gave them to my mother.

That fight was the first of countless others. They fought often, and for the life of me, I could not figure out why. They argued about the least little thing until one of them struck a wrong nerve and the fighting would begin. The police were called repeatedly to that small, one-bedroom apartment, and I was embarrassed as the neighbors looked on and whispered.

I don't know exactly when their marriage began to sour or if it did begin to sour. What I do recall is my mother leaving the apartment on weekdays to "attend a meeting at the church" around the corner. Sometimes after she left, I took the three-block walk from the apartment to the church, and there was no one in sight; the church was always dark and the doors were locked. My detective-like snooping confirmed what I suspected — my mother was lying to my stepfather about her whereabouts, and at worst, cheating on him. That realization sent a chill through me, because if Teddy ever found out, there would be hell to pay.

One particular evening, I was babysitting my brother and Ma supposedly was attending a weeknight church meeting. After giving the baby his bottle and preparing to change his diaper, I found there was only one clean diaper left, and I panicked. Teddy was asleep and I did not dare wake him. By this time, my nerves were shot. If my stepfather had known there were no clean diapers, a fight would have started as soon as my mother came home, or he would have gone to the church looking for her. I couldn't handle that, so I had to do something. In my frazzled state, I dashed into the bathroom, ran a tub of hot water with mild detergent and Clorox, emptied the soiled diapers from the diaper pail into the tub, and scrubbed the load of diapers by hand. I hand-wrung each wet diaper as best as I could. The baby had fallen asleep, so I took that opportunity to rush around the corner to the public laundromat to dry the diapers. I prayed that the baby did not wake up before I got back. When the diapers were dry, I quickly scurried back to the apartment and put the clean diapers in the baby's drawer. Not much later, my mother came home, checked on the baby, casually got undressed, and went to bed — totally unaware of the trauma I had experienced in trying to protect her. But I never told anyone, because I did not want to do or say anything that would cause problems for her.

Just when I was hoping that things would get better, my life was about to change for the worse.

CHAPTER 4
A STEPFATHER'S LUST

I was thirteen years old and my brother was two when I noticed my stepfather staring at me the way no grown man should look at a child. This was the beginning of my nightmare. Teddy began making sexual advances toward me. The second my mother turned her back or left me alone at the apartment with her husband, the man I should have been able to trust like a father, he would begin his disgusting overtures — telling me how pretty I was, how I had a much better body than my mother, and what he wanted to do to me sexually, followed by his bribe to buy me pretty clothes and give me money, insisting that nobody would ever know. I was very conscious that my body was not that of a typical thirteen-year-old. I had inherited the same physique as the women in my family — large breasts, broad hips, and small but shapely legs. I was also keenly aware that any inappropriate behavior between a man and a woman always seemed to be the woman's fault. I had heard about older women blaming young girls — not boys or men — when encounters with them went wrong or too far. "She must have done something" or "you know how those 'fast' girls are," people would say. Neither my youth nor my stepfather's intimidation got in the way of what I knew for sure: What my stepfather was attempting to coax me to do was disgusting and downright wrong.

Teddy was tireless in his quest to have sex with me. He was not a stepfather at all. He was a slithering pervert, waiting for any opportunity to catch me alone. When he did manage to corner me, he talked nonstop about what he would do for me in return for sex. He assured me that I would not get pregnant. "I'll use a rubber," he would say. I wanted to vomit.

Once the sexual harassment began, I spent much of my time trying to figure out ways to avoid him and protect myself from my mother's husband, which proved to be no easy task. I slept in the open space of the living room on a pullout sofa bed, making it easy for him to view the silhouette of my budding body underneath the covers. Fortunately for me, he was a brick mason by trade and had to leave for work early each morning. My mother followed close behind to allow adequate time on her way to work at a military base to drop the baby off at the babysitter. That was my only respite. I was home alone — free to bathe and dress for school — though not without a constant feeling of uneasiness and perpetual fear. I never knew what to expect. In my mind, Teddy could instantly appear, like a roach, out of nowhere. I did everything I could do to protect myself from being raped. I despised him.

The daily walk home from school was filled with agonizing dread, my mind continually racing, jam-packed with questions I could not answer. Why is this happening to me? What did I do? Who can I tell? Where can I hide? My life was a living hell, but my stepfather was not my only horror. My mother was at home in the evenings after work, something that, under normal circumstances, would be ideal for a young girl, but not for me. With no exceptions and no excuses, my daily responsibility after school was to clean the duplex apartment. The bed had to be made, dishes washed, floors swept, and furniture dusted. The apartment had to be spotless when she walked through the door. I made every effort to keep the apartment the way she expected it to be, but my mother was in no way a tidy person. Within minutes after she arrived home from work, the apartment appeared as if I had not done anything. I tried my best to get and keep my mother's approval, but no matter what I did, it was never enough, and things kept getting worse.

Inclement weather sometimes prevented my stepfather from working on a construction site. On those days, the walk home from school was absolutely torturous. As I got closer to the apartment, I would look for his car. If I spotted it parked in front of the apartment, I knew he was inside waiting to harass me, taunt me, and talk about having sex with me. If I did not go straight home, I would have to endure my mother's wrath about not cleaning the apartment, which could go on for hours. I felt trapped, knowing that regardless of what I decided to do, I was going to get pounced on by either my perverted stepfather or my angry mother. I was afraid to go home. I was between a rock and a hard spot.

One day my stepfather did not go to work, due to bad weather. After school, I decided to go to the home of a classmate who lived across the street from me with her grandmother. In the safety of their home, I kept a vigilant eye, looking through the living room window for my mother's car. When I saw her drive up and park, I, like a whirlwind, dashed from my classmate's home, ran across the street and upstairs into the apartment, and started cleaning as fast as I could. "Where the hell have you been? Why your sorry ass ain't cleaned this damn house?" My mother began a tongue-lashing that no self-respecting adult could stand to hear, much less a scared teenager, while my stepfather sat smugly on the sofa with a smirk on his face. My mother angrily screamed, "You ain't gon never be nothing and you ain't gon have nothin' but a houseful of babies!" Any effort to explain why I did not come straight home or why I neglected my chores would fall on deaf ears, and rightfully so, because I had made up lie after lie to avoid telling my mother the truth about what was happening to me. Although once I did attempt to tell her what kind of man she had married, on the day I learned from our next-door neighbor that my stepfather made an unwelcome pass at her. I told my mother what the neighbor said. "I don't believe that!" she snapped.

That was the end of it. My mother refused to hear another word, so I already knew the depth of her denial. She did not want to hear anything negative that I or anybody else had to say about her husband. I was stuck in the darkest hellhole that kept getting deeper and darker. There was no other choice but to accept my mother's tongue-whippings — cursing, yelling, and belittling — when all I was attempting to do was stay out of harm's way. I was a young girl in pain who needed help, so I reached out to someone safe and outside of my dysfunctional family — my dear, sweet godmother, Miss Maye.

Miss Maye was naturally nurturing and patient. She was a good listener, a hard worker, and always kind, generous, and gentle. She had one weakness that I knew of — she was pitifully head-over-heels in love with my father. Miss Maye always allowed herself to be a doormat for him, and at times, Daddy talked to her like she was garbage. I cannot remember Miss Maye ever standing up to him. He took merciless advantage of her. She cooked for him, cleaned his apartment, washed his clothes, loaned him money, and slept with him whenever he decided to have sex with her. She behaved as if it was a privilege to be with my father. Yet, Daddy viewed her as unworthy of his affection. Her trademark was a cheap black wig that for some reason was always lopsided on her head. According to Daddy, Miss Maye was not his type — she was not the trophy type he was accustomed to parading around in public, the type he could show off to his hustler friends. She not only knew how Daddy felt, but she had seen him frequently in the company of young beautiful women. Of course, his affairs hurt her immensely, but she remained silent and continued to accept his verbal, mental, and emotional abuse. Whatever he wanted or needed from her, she was right there at his beck and call. No sooner had he gotten what he needed from her than he was off to spend his time and money, as long as it lasted, on his bevy of women until he again needed Miss Maye. She was always waiting with open arms — open everything, including her checkbook. She was the kind of person who would help anyone in need, including her children, her family, my father, and me.

I told Miss Maye about the torture my stepfather was putting me through — not because I thought she could put an end to it. I did not allow myself to even think that my godmother could save me from my nightmare world, especially when she accepted my father's disrespect, abuse, and torment. I just needed to tell somebody about my predicament. I chose my godmother because I knew I could trust her. She was sympathetic, and at the same time, livid about what was happening to me. But what made all the difference in the world to me was that she believed every word I told her about Teddy. I asked her not to tell anyone and she kept her promise; however, she went out of her way to spend more time with me, and encouraged my father to take on a bigger role in my life. Outside of Miss Maye, there was no one else I could turn to.

A Stepfather's Lust

Who would I dare confide in and feel certain they would not reveal my secret? There was no one.

I was scared and alone. And then Pidgeon entered my world.

CHAPTER 5
MY FIRST LOVE

I was fourteen when I met Leonard Lawson as I walked home one day from Browne Junior High in Northeast Washington, DC, which was situated among a cluster of three other schools — Charles Young Elementary, Spingarn High, and Phelps Vocational High. He looked handsome and authoritative, standing on a hill that overlooked the schools. He was a high-ranking Phelps cadet, a status that magnified his natural leadership style. He fascinated me; his appeal for me was his self-confidence. That day, he was dressed in his cadet uniform, adorned with shiny gold medals. As I reached the top of the hill, he stopped me and asked, "What's your name?"

"Nesa," I said.

"What school do you go to?"

"Browne," I replied.

"Can I walk you home?" he asked.

"If you want to," I said.

Everyone called him Pidgeon. He was born and raised in New York by relatives before moving to Washington to live with his mother, stepfather, stepbrother, and stepsisters. Pidgeon told me that he had seen me many times leaving school and had wanted to talk to me for a long time.

After our first meeting, Pidgeon walked me home from school every day, a contrast to my dangerous walks home before I met him. I appreciated his walking me home because this put a stop to the torment I received every day after school from a gang of girls because I was light-skinned. When we reached my apartment, we would stand outside and talk briefly before I had to dash upstairs to clean the apartment before my mother arrived home. I liked Pidgeon, but my stepfather did not, which came as no surprise. He objected to and chased away any boy who paid attention to me. Oddly enough, my mother disagreed with my stepfather, telling him, "There is nothing wrong with Nesa having a friend." Because of her approval, Pidgeon and I became steady friends. Although he never came right out and asked, over time, it was understood that I was his girlfriend. As long as I did my chores and was in place to take care of my baby brother when my mother needed me, she allowed me to spend time with Pidgeon, who lived less than a ten-minute walk from where I lived. We went everywhere together — to the movies, the skating rink, restaurants, and to his home where we played music, danced, and hung out with his sisters, brother, and other neighborhood kids. Pidgeon was the first love of my young life and I lost my virginity to him. In my immature mind, I knew we would be together for life. Everything was perfect for us, at first.

Like my father, I found that Pidgeon was drawn to the thug life, which was a part of the environment we lived in, with hustlers, stick-up boys, gambling, and turf rivals. Many young black males turned to illegal activity to make fast money, buy new cars, and pull young girls. It was how they identified manhood. Pidgeon wanted to be the head of his own gang. He took pleasure in being a leader, making decisions, and carrying out plans with his "homeboys." He reveled in the admiration of his followers and enjoyed being feared and having his orders followed. Fully aware of all of that, I still desired his company and basked in his undivided attention, the warmth of his strong arms, and his tender kisses. I felt safe and secure when I was with him and felt privileged to be his girlfriend; therefore, I confided in him about my secret life of sexual torment from my stepfather. I repeated verbatim the vulgar things he said to me, and what he wanted to do to me, telling Pidgeon everything. I was certain Pidgeon would be beside himself with anger and would find a way to help me. I believed him when he told me he loved me and would never let anybody hurt me.

Shockingly, his reaction to my revelation was nowhere near what I expected. He shrugged off the news of my stepfather's sexual advances. "You shouldn't be surprised at what a man says or wants from a girl who is phat as you; just ignore him." I was crushed that my boyfriend thought what my stepfather was doing was no big deal. What he indicated was that "he was just being a man." So, reality set in again; help was nowhere to be found when it came to my stepfather's sexual advances. Although I was disappointed and hurt by Pidgeon's response, I remained in the relationship because I could not envision life without him.

Within a year of confiding in Pidgeon, his behavior began to change toward me — another dose of mind-boggling confusion. He became disrespectful and cruel. I recall being on a crowded bus on a Saturday afternoon, seated on the right side, close to the exit door. Pidgeon and his two homeboys were three seats behind me on the opposite side. Without any provocation on my part, Pidgeon started shouting, "Hey, you, Nesa. Tell everybody how much you love me." I didn't respond and sat frozen in my seat, wishing I could disappear. "Tell them," he demanded. He started hurling insults, making a scene at my expense for the people on the bus, but mostly for his homeboys. I ignored him. Humiliated and embarrassed, I nervously rang the bell to exit the bus at the next stop. Leaping up from my seat and scurrying to the exit door, I anxiously waited for the bus to stop to escape the confusing and embarrassing ordeal. Pidgeon persistently shouted obscenities at me until I was off the bus. I was dumbfounded, pondering to the point of exhaustion what I could have done to make my boyfriend become disrespectful, hateful, and hurtful. As hard as I tried, I couldn't figure it out. After that incident, I saw him very infrequently. On a few occasions, we saw see each other while visiting mutual friends or if we happened to be at the same party. Not long after the bus incident, I learned that Pidgeon changed toward me because he was dating another girl. Instead of telling me the truth, he took the coward's way out to end our relationship.

Pidgeon went on with his life and eventually married the girl that he was seeing when we were dating. A few years later, during an altercation at a drug store in Northeast Washington, DC, he was shot and paralyzed from his waist down. As a result of an infection in his legs, he died at the age of 27.

CHAPTER 6
THE SECRET IS REVEALED

The home of my classmate's kind grandmother was my refuge during my secret crisis. If my stepfather happened to be home when I arrived from school, I ran to her apartment and used her home as a safe haven until my mother arrived home from work.

There were times when I knew that my classmate's grandmother wanted to ask what was going on with me, but I never intended to reveal my shameful secret to her. However, one day after school, she point-blank asked me, "What's wrong?" By then, I was so tired, so beaten down, so desperate for help that I tearfully poured out the entire sordid mess. "Nesa, you have got to tell your mother," she said. I told her I couldn't — and for a while, I didn't. But she persisted, urging me to confide in my mother about what was happening to me with my stepfather.

Finally, I summoned the courage to tell my mother the truth — the whole truth. We were home alone when I walked timidly into the dining area and sat down at the table across from my mother. "Ma," I said with a lump in my throat, "I got something to tell you."

She gazed at me from across the table. "What is it?" she asked. With my insides cringing, I told my mother what no woman would want to hear about her husband, and worse, what he was doing to her child. She showed little emotion while I was talking to her, but apparently suspected that I was telling the truth. To my surprise, she called the police. There are no words to describe the relief I felt when a white female detective knocked at the door. My mother opened the door and greeted the detective, who was brunette, of average height, and dressed in plain clothes. Ma led her upstairs to the small dining area and we sat down at the table.

"What's going on?" the detective asked in a no-nonsense voice.

Without any hesitation, I spilled the entire sordid story to the detective as my mother listened. Once there was nothing left for me to say, the detective asked, matter-of-factly, "Has he ever penetrated you?"

"What?" I asked, not sure what she meant by "penetrated."

"Has he ever put his penis inside of you?" the detective asked.

"No," I said quickly. "He just always talked about wanting to do that to me."

"Well," the detective said, directing her full attention to my mother, "because he has not penetrated her, there has been no real crime. There's nothing I can do."

I sat in disbelief. My stepfather was not going to be punished. He was not going to jail. He was going to be free to abuse me for as long as we lived under the same roof. The detective stood, walked nonchalantly down the stairs, and closed the door behind her. After she left, my mother called her twin sister, Aunt Beth, to tell her that we were coming over. In fact, there was nowhere else she could think to go because she was an extremely private person who kept her family life close to the vest. And even if she had repaired her broken relationship with Aunt Constance, which she hadn't, my mother would have never disclosed the situation to the family gossiper. With her image at stake, it was important that the family continue to believe she had it all. My mother could not allow anyone, except her trusted twin sister, to discover that the man she married was a despicable child molester.

When we arrived at Aunt Beth's apartment, she and my mother talked privately in the bedroom while I remained in the living room. My stepfather called asking to speak with my mother, but apparently she was too upset or angry, and refused to take his call. My mother and I stayed at the apartment with Aunt Beth and Loretta that night, while Teddy rang the phone incessantly, pleading with my mother to return home, promising her they could work it out. I later learned he shifted the blame onto me, convincing my mother that I was jealous of them and was trying to break them up. "I've been a good husband to you," he lamented. "Everybody in this family knows how good I've been to you and our son. I treat

Nesa just like she is mine. And look what she's trying to do — break us up!"

The next day I watched in confusion as my mother gathered up her scant personal belongings, picked up her purse, and returned to the apartment she shared with her perverted, cheating, abusive, lying husband — leaving me with Aunt Beth and Loretta.

Although I still desired to be with my mother, I was more content to stay with Aunt Beth and Loretta than in that hellhole with my stepfather prowling and sniffing around me like a dog in heat. A few days later, my mother telephoned my aunt to tell her that she was coming to pick me up. It was not long before she arrived at the apartment, ushered me into the car, and drove me right back to that hellish place I prayed I never had to see again.

After I returned home, I never so much as heard a word from my mother about his sexual behavior toward me — it was like it never happened. Although, to my knowledge, she had only shared what happened with Aunt Beth, somehow the secret was revealed and quickly snaked its way through the family like wildfire. What I heard through the grapevine was, "Teddy said that Nesa wasn't doing nothing but trying to break up their marriage because she's jealous." But nobody ever asked me what happened.

What I shall never forget is that I was viewed as the "troublemaker" by most family members. I was not given an iota of moral support from anyone in the family— not my mother or her sisters. My stepfather was shown compassion and understanding, and given support by the majority of the family. The most painful blow came when troublemaker Aunt Constance cast her support for my stepfather. What's worse is that she blatantly lied, knowing that I never mentioned anything to her about Teddy. "Nesa told me from her own mouth that she made the whole thing up," she falsely reported to the family That's the kind of vicious, vindictive, lying woman she was. She is now deceased, but I still struggle to forgive her for that lie.

Living with my mother — something I had constantly dreamed about — had become a continuous nightmare. I went from feeling desperate to hopeless. I was left with no choice but to seek help from my gangster father. I asked Daddy if I could live with him, and he said yes. My mother had no objection. I believe she told him her conjured-up version of the story, whatever that was.

On the drive to his apartment, it was apparent that my father was bothered about what had happened to me. He always told me, "A man ain't nothin'." But by this time, I was barely hanging onto what was left of my sanity. I was a fifteen-year-old girl praying and hoping for the nightmare to end.

CHAPTER 7
LIVING WITH DADDY

Carrying a stuffed suitcase filled with hastily packed clothes, I followed Daddy into the small one-bedroom apartment he shared with Margaret Tidewell, his current girlfriend, who was living with lupus, a chronic illness. She gave me a welcome embrace that was filled with affection and tenderness. What was different about Margaret was that somehow she managed to actually live with my father in his apartment. Usually he preferred to live alone, so the arrangement was quite foreign to me. Outside of Miss Maye, Margaret was the closest thing to an angel I had thus far encountered. In that moment, I felt a calm relief to be safely away from my stepfather. It didn't matter that Margaret was as kind as any human being could be; my father was extremely strong-willed, stubborn, opinionated, and selfish. So, whatever relief I felt vanished faster than the evaporation of dew.

Daddy was uncomfortable with me living with him and over time we both became uncomfortable. I consciously strived not to be a burden to him, to keep out of his way, to be virtually invisible — something I had a lot of practice doing with my mother and stepfather. I tiptoed carefully around his one-bedroom apartment, cognizant that I did not fit into his world. The truth is nobody did because he was accustomed to his freedom and appreciated not having to be responsible for a family.

But it was my father's painfully insensitive use of words that cut like a knife, revealing his chauvinistic, misogynistic view of women. Daddy's raw comments stung like a swarm of bees and served as a sobering reminder of his insensitivity to other people's feelings, especially those closest to him. There was one particular characteristic that I grew to abhor — his belief that a woman was supposed to obey a man. His mantra was "the man is the boss. If a woman talks back to a man, and she don't do what he tells her to do, he ought to beat her." He believed that if a woman did not listen to her man, she should be punished. He also wanted to make sure I understood how men think when it comes to women. One day while riding in his car, he said, "You're a big girl now. You can't be walking around men unless you're covered up. Men ain't shit. Men don't want but one thing from you."

There were times when I saw him become irate simply because some-one disagreed with him. Disagreeing with him on anything brought on a tsunami. He would get so angry that his veins would bulge on both sides of his head and his blood pressure would shoot sky-high. On several of his tantrum-throwing episodes, I thought he would have a stroke.

The depth of my father's uncontrollable rage was confirmed in a story told to me by my Aunt Eunice. According to her, after I was born, he be-lieved my mother was cheating on him. Crazy with jealousy one night, he went to her house and accused her of being with another man. In his rage, he broke off a wooden leg from a nearby chair and hit her in the head so hard that it almost cracked her skull. She told me that it was a miracle that my mother survived the assault. Ma always said, "That man's crazy."

Of course, I didn't have to wonder if any or part of what Aunt Eunice said was true. I had already seen Daddy's cruel treatment of two women in his life: my godmother, Miss Maye, and his current girlfriend, Mar-garet.

Margaret was the first and the last woman to live with my father. He spoke to her in a harsh, hateful, and disrespectful manner. He was always putting her down and accusing her of sleeping with other men, even though she didn't leave the apartment without him except to go to work. The poor woman couldn't do anything right or well enough to please him. Without any shadow of doubt, my father sincerely believed a woman should accept her place — behind him; and he kept his women in check with intimidation, threats, and emotional, mental, and physical abuse.

Ironically, throughout my life, one relationship after another, every man that I would live with or marry, with few exceptions, would possess some, if not most, of the same character traits as my father.

Nothing would demonstrate more vividly how cold my father could be than when lupus began to take its toll on Margaret, requiring her to need special assistance. My father didn't show Margaret the least bit of compassion. He no longer wanted her around him, and told her that she had to find another place to live. As mean as he was, he had deep phobias about germs and illnesses. Margaret, being the passive soul that she was, did not put up an argument. Like Miss Maye, she only wanted to please her man, so as soon as she found a place to live, Margaret sadly left. Daddy effortlessly moved forward with his life and continued to enjoy the company of young women. However, in an effort most likely to assuage his guilt, Daddy would visit Margaret briefly and give her money to help her along. He believed money could fix everything, but soon found that money could not fix Margaret. She died less than a year later.

With all that I heard, all that I knew, and all that I had seen with my own eyes, I still looked for the good in my father. For example, he never cursed in front of me or called me out of my name like my mother did. He was good to his aging parents, sending them money and paying to have an indoor bathroom built on the back of their country house. He let me go to South Carolina to spend summers with Grandma Mamie and Grandpa Neb, and bought me ice cream and pretty clothes. He wasn't all bad, couldn't be all bad; he was my daddy. I needed to see the good instead of acknowledging and accepting what was staring me straight in the face — the truth. Yet, no matter how hard I searched for the good in him, or how deeply in denial I sank, the ugly side of my father was alive and well. Daddy could be cordial and polite one minute, and angry, impatient, and cutting the next. His harsh, bitter tongue and his mercurial, hateful mood swings were burdensome. Never knowing what to expect from him, I clearly understood what my boundaries were in his world. I had to get out. Within a span of weeks, I decided to return to my mother. She did not object to my decision to move back home. In my fifteen-year-old brain, I rationalized that one hell was no worse than the other. It seemed I was going to go crazy no matter where I was.

Living with Daddy

I returned to the apartment with my mother and stepfather, still craving a relationship with my mother because I still wanted her love and her approval. I wanted to be near her and I wanted her to want me near. My stepfather was an awful bastard, but at least now the whole truth was out, whether the family believed me or not. My mother knew; her sisters, brothers, and my father knew. My godmother, Miss Maye, knew and believed me. For all the good that it did me, the police knew. In my mind, there was no doubt that my stepfather would now walk a straight line.

But my confidence crumbled within a month of returning home. Nothing had changed; in fact, he became more determined than ever to convince me to sleep with him. Once again, I was back to having to figure out ways to survive. This time there was absolutely no one I could turn to for help. I was totally alone, with school being my only respite. I couldn't concentrate on much of anything and envied my classmates who I thought lived normal, peaceful, civilized lives.

One night as I was cleaning the kitchen, my stepfather propositioned me the way he had on other occasions. But that night, something inside of me snapped. I grabbed a knife off of the counter, whirled around, pointed it at him, and growled through gritted teeth, "Nobody might have believed me the last time, but it won't matter if they don't believe me this time. If you as much as come near me, I'll stab you in your fuckin' heart." He gazed at me with amusement, laughed an evil, wicked, demonic laugh, and slowly backed out of the kitchen. That was the last time he approached me in the duplex apartment.

CHAPTER 8
TEEN PREGNANCY
A SOBERING EXPERIENCE

Waiting for life to end, I was a walking zombie. Then, almost like divine intervention, I became friends with a boy who had recently moved into the neighborhood. His name was Jeremy Willie Wilson, Jr. but he was known as Pop.

We walked to school every morning and walked home every evening together. I spent a good deal of time at Pop's house because I didn't want to be around my stepfather. Teddy did not like Pop, although he was as different from Pidgeon as night is from day. He was tall, dark, and very handsome with beautiful, even, white teeth and sexy dimples that stood out when he smiled. Unlike Pidgeon, Pop had no interest in the thug life. He was a kind, funny, dependable person from a respectable family. Pop's father was an Army master sergeant and his mother was a typical southern wife from Sarasota, Florida. She did not have a high level of education and spent most of her time as a homemaker. I adored his parents and loved spending as much time with them as I could. How I marveled at the relationship Pop had with them — his father, his mother, sister, and brother; they were happy and genuinely enjoyed being together.

Whenever I was with Pop, I felt loved, not dirty and nasty the way my stepfather made me feel. I believed that Pop sincerely cared about me; it was important that I believed that. Somebody had to care about me, and at that time, he was the only person who gave me a safe place to escape from my insane world. In the moments I spent with Pop, I could pretend that my stepfather didn't exist, pretend my life was normal.

After a few too many quiet moments alone with Pop, I found myself fifteen, pregnant, and terrified. So, I did what any average, terrified fifteen-year old girl would do — I hid it. But on an unforgettable Sunday evening, I went into the kitchen where my mother was preparing pork ribs for dinner. I was already feeling nauseous, and the smell of the spareribs baking in the oven sent me hurling into the bathroom. I quickly cleaned up, rinsed out my mouth, and went back into the kitchen. My mother was not fooled and the secret was out. "You're pregnant, aren't you?" she asked, standing near me. "I think so," I said, petrified, but relieved that she now knew. "When was the last time you had your period?" she asked. I didn't answer. I stood there with my eyes glued to the floor. I knew she couldn't wait to call my father and I literally wanted to just die.

* * *

My father knocked on the door and walked up the stairs, through the small dining area, and into the kitchen where I was nervously washing dishes. Less than twenty-four hours earlier, I stood facing my mother; now it was Daddy that I had to face. "You done messed up your life," he said, each word coated with disappointment, hurt, and anger. "That boy ain't thinking 'bout you." I didn't say a word and lowered my head in shame, but could sense him glaring at me. "You are going to have this baby, and you are going to take care of it. This is the life you chose! You made your bed — now you lie in it." I didn't dare look up, I just couldn't.

While Never Duncan, Jr., may not have been the model father, he always held onto a dream for me to be highly educated. I would eventually learn that he expected his daughter to become a politician, an accomplishment that certainly would have been a way for me to gain his admiration. It would have given him a reason to be proud of his daughter and a way to make me feel good about myself. But what he wanted for me — a career in politics — interested me about as much as playing the piano. The problem was that it was his dream, not my dream. My dream was to have a happy family with a good husband. However, on that day, what I wanted didn't matter. What mattered was what my father wanted; and from where he stood, I had thrown his dream right out the window. Daddy did not believe in abortions, so in eight months I would become an unwed mother — making his daughter unfit to hold any political office. Daddy had made his decision that I was having the baby and I was going to take care of it. That would be my punishment for destroying his dream.

Daddy turned to leave, and I listened to his footsteps as he slowly walked away. I hesitantly lifted my head and stared at his back, normally strong, erect, and proud, now hunched over with the weight of disappointment. I watched him descend the stairs and vanish from sight, closing the apartment door behind him. Understanding the hurt and disappointment I caused my father and how badly I let him down burned a hole in my heart. If I managed to sleep a wink that night, it was from pure mental exhaustion.

Early the next morning, I went into the dining area and sat down at the table, alone with my thoughts in absolute silence. A short while later, my mother came in and sat at the table with me. Sitting in utter silence for what seemed like an eternity, I felt so stupid — sick and terrified. My mother suddenly broke the silence by saying, "The best thing for you to do is to have an abortion."

"I don't want to have an abortion," I said. "I want to have the baby."

My mother took a deep breath and in painstaking detail laid out what my life would be like and what would happen to me if I had a baby so young with no education and no way of providing support. "Who's going to take care of it, because I damn sure ain't. Your friends are going to be out there having fun, going to parties, and what are you going to be doing? You're going to be stuck in this house with a baby, because I done told you many times I'm not taking care of no babies. You're going to get big, fat, and out of shape, and that boy that got you pregnant is going to move on to another pretty girl who'll still have her figure." Maintaining a good figure was on the top of her "extremely important" list. She always reminded me to "wear a girdle to keep your stomach flat."

That night, as I lay in bed in the darkness of my room, sick with nausea, I could not escape the look of disappointment, disgust, and anger on my father's face. He had made what he wanted perfectly clear — he expected me to have the baby and I was going to be the person to take care of it. I knew from taking care of my brother the time and responsibility required to take care of a baby. In the deafening quiet, I could not shut out the words my mother drilled into my head — she did not want me bringing a baby into her house, I was going to get big and fat, Pop was going to move on to another pretty girl with a figure. I was bombarded with thoughts of my father's expectation and my mother's warning about life as a teenage mother.

I took care of my brother, but he was not my baby even though sometimes I felt like I was his mother. I lost count of the number of times he had to tag along with me when I really didn't feel like being bothered. I resented having to be responsible for him when I wanted to hang out with my friends or be alone. I seriously thought about what was required to care for a baby based on caring for my brother — bathing, feeding, dressing, and walking him when he was sick. Simply taking him to the park, or watching him when my mother wasn't at home or was too busy, was a whole different ball game from having the sole physical, financial, and emotional responsibility for another human being. I could give my brother back to his mother, but with my own child, there would be no handoff. Then I thought of my friends who were now teenage parents and could not go to parties and picnics because they didn't have a babysitter. Those girls watched their babies' fathers with other girls — never visiting them or providing financial assistance. Boys would not want to date a girl with a baby. My mind replayed the drama that would be my destiny. In the morning, I knew what I had to do. Violently nauseous and in bed when my mother came out of her bedroom, I was absolutely sure I did not want to be sick and pregnant.

"I want to have the abortion," I said.

My mother didn't attempt to hide her relief, and wasted no time making the necessary arrangements to have my pregnancy terminated. Within a day or two, she drove me to a rundown apartment building in the proj-

Teen Pregnancy

ects in Southeast. The outside appearance of the apartment was what one would have expected to see in a typical ghetto neighborhood inhabited by people who were economically disadvantaged.

We entered through the front of the building and climbed a flight of smelly, dingy stairs to an apartment on the second floor. My mother knocked on the door and an attractive, nicely dressed lady in her mid-thirties invited us inside. The apartment bore no resemblance to the grungy outside; I was amazed. It was as if I walked into a miniature palace. It was nothing short of the elegance expected in a fashionable home of the "rich and famous" — fine furniture, plush carpet, and spot-less — so clean it could have easily passed the white-glove test. I re-member thinking to myself, "Why would someone with so much money live in the projects?" Years later, I would learn that the person who per-formed my illegal abortion was a nurse who did abortions on the side. But like most people who engage in illegal activity, it was necessary to keep it underground and inconspicuous.

My mother took a seat in the living room while the lady led me into a bedroom and instructed me to remove my clothes from the waist down. She told me to lie face up on the bed and then she left the room. A short while later, the abortionist returned carrying strange instruments. She in-structed me to spread my legs apart, and used one of the instruments to open my vagina. She began inserting a rubber tube, supported and guided by an unraveled wire coat hanger, deep into my uterus. I felt a sharp pain that lingered for several seconds. The abortionist then removed the coat hanger, leaving the rubber tube inside, and told me to get dressed. She quietly left the room.

I went into the living room where my mother was waiting. The abor-tionist was explaining what to expect as a result of the procedure. I vividly remember her saying, "In a couple of hours Nesa will begin to miscarry." I recall following my mother out of the immaculate apart-ment, down the flight of smelly, dingy stairs, and getting into the car, and my mother driving off. But instead of taking me home, which is what I expected, she took me to Aunt Beth's apartment and — without a kiss, hug, or any show of affection — left me in her care. I had no idea of the hell I was about to experience.

For a couple of hours I felt fine; then, as predicted, I began to miscarry. My aunt put me to bed, where I lay doubled over in excruciating pain for too many unbelievably agonizing hours. At first the bleeding was light, but soon became heavier with thick red clots. The bleeding became so heavy that Aunt Beth had to change my pad practically every few minutes. She feverishly tried to stop the hemorrhaging, but when the bleeding did not lessen, Aunt Beth, by now visibly distraught, called my mother. Wracked with pain, I could hear the fear in her voice. "We need to get this girl to a hospital."

The relentless pain and loss of blood caused me to lose consciousness. Miraculously, I awoke to blessed daylight the next morning. Thanks to the Creator, the hemorrhaging had stopped and it was the most beautiful day I had ever seen — the sun brightly shining and birds singing outside the window. After all the pain, suffering, physical weakness, and mixture of emotions, I believed that I was experiencing one of God's divine miracles. He had given me another chance at life. I was alive — and starving. Fortunately, Aunt Beth was preparing a light breakfast for me. I remember thinking how lucky and grateful I was to be alive.

Two days passed before my mother came to take me home. It was the first time I had seen or talked to her since she left me in the care of Aunt Beth. After I gathered my belongings, we left and rode home in absolute silence. My mother never talked to me about the abortion, the hemorrhaging that almost took my life, her absence, or the reason for it. Except for Aunt Beth, no one in the family reached out to me. I don't know when or how my father found out about the abortion, but he never mentioned it to me. The only other person who offered me solace was Pop, who never stopped calling to check on me while I was with Aunt Beth.

With the abortion behind me, I had an epiphany: A happy family for me did not include children. To make sure I would never be in that predicament again, I immediately scheduled an appointment with the doctor and asked for birth control. The fact that my life was in danger and that I almost died as a result of the decision to terminate an unplanned and unwanted pregnancy helped both me and Pop to grow up quickly. We both knew that we could not allow that to happen again. Pop and I found our way back to sharing time together, laughing, talking over the phone, partying, and visiting with each other. Only this time we were cognizant of the consequences of careless, unprotected sex. We were closer friends than ever, but I still had to deal with my stepfather.

CHAPTER 9
GOD ANSWERS MY PRAYER

In the spring of 1966, my mother and Teddy purchased a detached, single-family, three-bedroom house. I was relieved to be in a larger house with my very own bedroom with a door to close. Almost everything changed except I still lived with the same damn stepfather. After being in the house close to one year, my mother and stepfather planned a New Year's Eve party. In the kitchen preparing for their first holiday party in their new home, my mother realized she did not have any pickle relish to make potato salad, and she asked my stepfather to drive me to the store to get it. I was shocked…speechless. I could not believe my mother — after everything she knew, everything we had gone through — would send me anywhere alone with her husband. Even if she believed I was a liar (in her heart, she knew I told her the truth), believed I had made up the whole ugly story, I could not understand why she put me in such a volatile situation. Many times I asked myself why she did not ask him to go to the store alone. She knew that I made it my business not to go near him. I reluctantly left the house and got in the car with him to go to the store. I sat frozen in my seat, wrapped tightly in my new brown suede coat, staring out of the passenger window, unable to move, unable to fathom the position my mother put me in for some damn pickle relish.

We were halfway to the 7-Eleven when my stepfather started with his same old dirty tactics — saying that he wouldn't get me pregnant and would give me money to buy whatever I wanted. By this time, I was nervous to the point that when we got to the store, I inadvertently purchased sweet pickles instead of pickle relish. Teddy barely parked the car in front of the house when I hastily jumped out, ran in the house, and handed the brown paper bag to my mother. She took one look at what I had bought and flipped out — cursing, screaming, belittling me. "That's not what I asked you to get!" she shouted. "I told you to get me some pickle relish! You can't do a damn thing right. Go right on back out there and get me what I told you to get…pickle relish!"

On the way back to the 7-Eleven, my stepfather didn't say a word to me. Quietly I sat frozen in my seat with quivering insides, until we reached the store again. We rode back in the same sickening silence. Jumping out of the car again after it was parked, I ran in the house and straight to the kitchen and handed my mother the jar of pickle relish.

Thundering up the stairs to my bedroom, I closed the door, dropped down on my knees, and prayed. My prayer was simple: "God, please take me or him. I don't care which one of us you take — just take one of us, because I can't live like this anymore." I prayed to God to die. I was not afraid to die. Whichever one of us God chose to take was fine with me, but one of us had to go.

Early the next morning, New Year's Day 1967, my stepfather cracked open my bedroom door, poked his head in, and with his sneaky grin said he was going to the market. "You want to ride with me?" he asked. "Get out of my room!" I snapped. He laughed that wicked, demonic laugh that made my skin crawl, and then said, "I'm taking Chris with me." Chris was my beautiful German shepherd puppy. "Leave my dog here!" I angrily retorted. He laughed again as he was going down the stairs and out of the house. About an hour had passed when the phone rang. My mother answered and I heard her scream. I ran to the top of the stairs as I heard her screaming and crying.

"What's wrong, Ma?"

"Teddy's been in an accident on 295," she cried hysterically. "I have to get to the hospital — somebody take me to the hospital!" All that I remember is that someone took her to the hospital to see about her sorry-ass husband.

A few members of my stepfather's family had spent the night at our house after the New Year's Eve party. Teddy's sister later told me that he crashed his car on I-295 trying to avoid hitting a dog. How coincidental! Shortly after my mother arrived at the hospital, my stepfather died from cardiac arrest. My mother was hysterical and I was ecstatic. God had answered my prayer. At his wake, I touched the cold body with my finger to make sure he was really dead. He was. I remember asking myself, "What am I supposed to do now? Do I cry? Do I scream? Do I laugh?" I did what I learned to do best — I faked a cry, all the while feeling nothing but blessed relief. My prayer had been answered. God had chosen my stepfather and set me free.

CHAPTER 10

MOTHER STARTS OVER

Nineteen hundred and sixty-seven — at the age of forty-one, wedding bells rang a second time for my mother. Less than one year after Ma buried Teddy, she married Herman Spelman (Thrift), who was thirty-four years old — seven years her junior. He had never been married, but it was not long before she described him as a worthless, lazy-ass man. "He just don't have no git-up-and-go" was her never-ending complaint. Thrift and my mother were coworkers for years at the same military hospital, and I found it odd that she married him shortly after Teddy died. I didn't know what to make of that situation, although I knew she had a fear of being alone. In her world, it was better to have half of a man than no man at all.

Thrift was a man who liked to eat, sleep, and drink liquor. He was a dedicated worker and an alcoholic. Before he married my mother, he was living in a rented room in a rowhouse in Northwest DC near North Capitol Street. An old car was literally all he had to show for his many years of work at Walter Reed Hospital. Thrift was diagnosed with cirrhosis, a liver disease often caused by alcohol abuse, well before they were married. The doctors warned him to stop drinking or he would surely die. To help him overcome alcoholism, he entered a rehabilitation center for a few months. Many of my mother's dates with him were spent at the rehabilitation center, which was run by the Veterans Administration in West Virginia. When he was released from the rehabilitation center, he never touched a drop of liquor again, nor did he return to his rented room. He lived with us from that day forward.

My mother married a man knowing that he had no desire to obtain more than what he had. What my mother already had was more than sufficient for him. She always desired the nicer things in life, strived to have more, and ultimately tried to bring Thrift closer to her way of thinking. When she suggested to him that they purchase their own new, more spacious home using his veteran's benefits, he flatly refused. "Why should I take on that kind of debt for another house when we can continue to live here? Ain't nothin' wrong with this house," he said.

Thrift was unbelievably cheap and selfish and would remain that way throughout their marriage. His absolute refusal to buy a new home for them was the nexus of my mother's disrespect for him. Life with him left her perpetually unhappy and unfulfilled. Even though she was utterly disappointed in Thrift, she maintained her role as the dutiful wife, a role deeply rooted in her southern upbringing.

On the positive side, living with my new stepfather was devoid of sexual torment. He never disrespected me in any way, had a pleasant demeanor, and was a good listener. This was the closest I had come to experiencing a functional family even though subtle dysfunction existed. Holidays and family gatherings were usually at our home because there was a basement and back yard. We were the picture of a happy family. It was the image my mother portrayed during her first marriage and she was hell-bent on continuing the façade in her second. The only people who knew the truth about how my mother really felt about Thrift and her life were her sisters and me.

CHAPTER 11
BABY BROTHER

Toby was becoming an intolerable nightmare with each passing year; my brother became too spoiled for anybody to handle. Of course, my mother was no help; in fact, she was his enabler. Toby could do no wrong. He was the apple of her eye. No one was allowed to correct her precious son and all the while he was becoming a terror. He was fully aware of his special position in the family and used it totally to his benefit. All he had to do was appear unhappy and my mother would give him whatever he wanted to change his mood. Not even complaints from teachers and other outsiders could convince her that he could do anything wrong — everyone was lying. He was the center of her world and he learned to be totally dependent on her. What Toby wanted, he got from my mother, and as he reached adulthood, from his women — no questions asked.

Unadulterated favoritism for my brother further damaged the already fragile relationship between my mother and me, and the relationship continued to deteriorate. It is obvious that I was not the only one affected by the relationships my mother had with men. Toby grew to become a vile and evil man. To this day, he lives his life expecting and demanding that women indulge his every whim. He expects women to cater to him and obey, because that is the way my mother raised him. Every single woman who has been in my brother's life has been disrespected and abused. As far as I know, to date, Toby has 14 children with multiple women, and provides little to no financial or emotional support for most of his seeds, perpetuating a vicious, crime-ridden cycle of poverty. Usually, by the time his women found the strength to leave him and move on to safer ground, they were emotionally, physically, mentally, and spiritually beaten down, almost to a point of no return.

By the time I was sixteen, I was angry and rebellious — so angry with my mother that I no longer cared if she saw any worth in me. I didn't care anymore. I lost respect and was still furious with her for ignoring the fact that Teddy, her first husband, made my life a living hell as a result of his sexual advances toward me.

Although I still wanted her love, I no longer worked to prove my worth. I was simply sick and tired of being sick and tired, ignored, and misunderstood. So, as usual, I looked for an escape and I found it: work.

CHAPTER 12

A TASTE OF INDEPENDENCE
AND A DIFFERENT SEXUAL HARASSMENT EXPERIENCE

At Ballou High School, I studied business so that I would be prepared to work after graduating. I was a star typist and stenographer and decided to get a part-time job after school, but needed a work permit and parental consent to participate in the city's youth employment program. I was forced to ask my mother for permission to work. Initially, she was completely against my getting a job because she said that working might get in the way of my schoolwork and cause my grades to drop. This was confusing to me because she never showed an interest in my education. I remember her going to maybe two PTA meetings. I would later learn that she had a strange need for people to be dependent on her. She was comfortable with Thrift and Toby, who made her feel important and useful because they were weak and dependent. It would be years before I realized how much alike we were in that regard.

From the time I was seven, I traveled alone by train to and from Woodruff, South Carolina, during the summers to visit my grandparents. Early on, life with my mother and her first husband caused me to become strong and independent. Having a job and making my own money would, in her eyes, just cause me to become "too independent." In my young mind, I needed a way to earn my own money because it would put me in a position to not need to ask my mother for anything or wait for my father to bring me "spending change." Despite my mother's resistance to my desire to work, I persisted until she reluctantly signed my work permit, providing me a new kind of freedom.

The DC Police Department offered me my first assignment at its Southwest precinct, in a program that allowed me to work no more than 20 hours per week. I looked forward to going to work — four hours after school each day — meeting interesting people, and learning work skills. Having a legitimate reason for being away from home and away from my pre-gangster brother was like having a slice of heaven. Work and school occupied my time, mind, and life, allowing me to forget, at least temporarily, about the unconditional love my mother freely showered on my brother while I watched, feeling rejected and neglected. Contrary to what my mother feared, my grades did not decline, but improved drastically. In fact, I became an honor student for the first time. Finally, my life was full of hope, anticipation, and excitement.

In my second assignment, I worked as a clerk typist with the Criminal Investigation Division (CID) near Capitol Hill, twenty hours a week during the school year and forty hours a week during the summer. I was thrilled to work full-time in the summer, and was a quick and eager study with excellent secretarial skills. Police officers and administrative staff were friendly and helpful. All was going well.

Filled with the pride of earning my own money and free from the mental torture of my mother's first husband, I began to feel my confidence and self-esteem improving. Life for me was looking up and changing day by day for the better. Little did I know another crisis was looming.

Captain Harris, head of the CID, was a pale, red-haired, middle-aged white man. At first, he seemed pleasant and kind, a fatherly type who I thought I could trust. One day he offered to pick up me and Regina, who attended a different high school, and drive us to work. She was a beautiful girl with caramel-brown skin who worked with me in the same department. As naïve teenagers, new to the world of work, we considered it a privilege to be picked up from school and driven to work by our boss in a shiny new Cadillac. Of course, Regina and I eagerly accepted his offer.

After a while, though, it got to a point that whenever we were alone, Captain Harris started to make unwelcome advances, sometimes asking me out after work. Unlike my mother's first husband, who was downright vulgar with his sexual advances, Captain Harris used a more subtle,

A Taste of Independence

but no less repulsive, approach. I was stunned. I could not believe this was happening to me again. "How do I handle rejecting a white man — an authority figure — without creating a catastrophe?" I asked myself. Propositioning me was a man who was old enough to be my father, or perhaps my grandfather and, because he was white had certain entitlements but the entitlements would not include me.

I used the "duck and dodge" tactic similar to that used with my stepfather to keep my distance from this old, white, disgusting pervert. Aware of the racial and gender conflicts in the late 1960s, I understood that white men only wanted one thing from Negro girls and women — sex. In their minds, we were immoral, sexual animals. My experience with Teddy taught me about the lust of men, and Captain Harris was not getting a damn thing, not from me. I developed an instant abhorrence for him and threw myself into my work, working so hard that at times it was hard for me to think about anything else. My attitude toward him made him angry and vindictive. In response to my rejection of him, he decided to show me just who was in charge.

Although I had been employed less than one year in the CID, officers and staff credited me with being innovative and creative. During that period, I created a schedule form for detectives in the division that improved the efficiency of the entire operation. One day immediately after I returned from lunch, Captain Harris called me into his office. In a few words, he fired me — offering no reason for his action. I quietly packed my personal belongings, and with my head held high, left the CID forever.

I still often wonder if Regina had the same experience with the captain as I did. If so, she never mentioned it to me, and I did not share my experience with her. I wonder if I would have been fired if I had told someone about Captain Harris's sexual harassment toward me. I wonder if anyone would have stood up for me, since I was considered such a great asset to the office. Or would my allegations about this so-called respectable white man with a high position on the force have been swept under the rug? I am confident that the incident would have been ignored, and I still would have been fired.

CHAPTER 13
FROM HIGH SCHOOL TO ADULTHOOD

On a beautiful, sunny morning in May 1969, clothed in my black cap and gown, I proudly marched across the stage in the packed Ballou High School gymnasium, grasping my high school diploma. A wide grin covered my face as I shook hands with Mr. Carlo, the school principal. I shared in the excitement with my classmates, exchanging hugs and kisses and promises to stay in touch. We all thought this day took forever to arrive. There was an obvious difference between my classmates' guests and mine. When I held up my diploma for all to see, my mother, stepfather, and brother were not in sight. But I knew my daddy was somewhere in the audience, although I was unaware of his presence until after the ceremony ended.

As I walked out of my high school for the last time among crowds of jubilant classmates, families, and friends, I saw Daddy standing amidst a throng of people alongside the building. I rushed over to him. "Hey girl," he said. We didn't embrace; that was not his style. "You've made it to first base," he said, and gave a broad, approving smile. That indescribable feeling I got whenever I managed to make Daddy smile overwhelmed me.

Daddy was unwavering when it came to my getting a good education, because he believed education was the only way to have a good life. He despised ignorance and weakness. On the day of my graduation, I felt proud of myself — proud that I had finally gotten it right in my father's eyes. I now possessed the one thing he had wanted for himself but never obtained — a high school diploma. I had achieved what no one in his family had. Yet, I got my biggest emotional boost from what I had waited to tell Daddy. Because of my top grades, class ranking, high-level clerical skills, and prior work experience, I had been recruited and hired by a nationally known education organization. As an entry-level secretary, my annual salary would be a whopping $4,911 — a big deal for an eighteen-year-old black girl in 1969. I would be earning more than my mother, who worked as a custodial engineer.

As a high school graduate, with a full-time job, and legally an adult, I could set my own rules. I was on cloud nine and ready to take charge of my own life. Two months after my graduation, I moved out of my mother's house and subleased a comfortable one-bedroom basement apartment from a co-worker who was getting married. The apartment was less than a block from my father's apartment.

But beneath the "got-it-going-on appearance" was a well-kept secret. I did not want to be alone. I still wanted — no, desperately needed — that one thing that seemed to elude me: a happy family. In my fairytale thoughts, come hell or high water, I was going to have a happy family. All I needed was a good husband, but the problem was I had no idea what characteristics made a good husband.

CHAPTER 14

MY FIRST HUSBAND

y husbands were all different — different family lives, religious beliefs, professions, hobbies, and social likes and dislikes. Some were quiet and reserved, while others were loud and aggressive. Some were lackadaisical, others were hardworking go-getters. In one way or another, all of my husbands were similar to the men who previously shaped my life: my insane stepfather who abused my mother and me; Pidgeon, who verbally and emotionally abused me; Uncle Gregory, who emotionally abused the woman who loved him; one-armed Uncle Cordell, who physically abused women; Uncle J.W., who fought Aunt Eunice on a weekly basis; Herman Spelman, who had absolutely no ambition in life except to live off of what my mother had accumulated before they married; Captain Harris, a white police captain and my supervisor who fired me for not accepting his unwelcome advances; and my hustler father, who was vicious and cruel toward the women in his life.

I learned how to interact with men from the women in my family, and took this learned behavior into relationships, and then marriage. My mother accepted physical, verbal, and emotional abuse from her first husband and emotional and financial abandonment from her quiet, recovering-alcoholic second husband for the sake of simply having a man. There was always drama with Aunt Beth as she fought with her married lover with the strength and fury of a man. Aunt Eunice suffered years of mental and physical torture at the hands of her husband. Miss Maye, my godmother, and Margaret Proctor, two of my father's many girlfriends, allowed him to mercilessly abuse them in every way.

When it came to men and relationships, I made more than enough poor choices. As my roller-coaster life continued to unfold, several men helped to shape and shatter my world.

***

Reginald (Reggie) Hardeman was my first husband and the one I never loved and should have never married. He was tall with a medium-caramel complexion, a beautiful smile, and dancing hazel eyes. I met Reggie, who had recently moved to Washington from North Carolina, through a mutual friend. He was single, and it was not too long before we began to spend most of our free time together. During the time we dated, there were instances when my plans did not include Reggie, and it was during those times that I noticed his jealousy, but ignored it, and we agreed to marry.

On September 11, 1972, on a hot Saturday afternoon at a small Baptist church in DC, I became Mrs. Nesa Chappelle Hardeman. While in my mother's bedroom putting the finishing touches on my makeup before leaving the house to go to the church, Grandma Mamie, who was sitting on the bed, looked up at me and said, "You will never be more beautiful than on this day."

It was a picture-perfect wedding — my smiling mother, father, family, and friends gathered for the occasion — the perfect ambience. My precious Grandma Mamie, who I wasn't sure would make the trip because of her age, did attend, which made everything perfect for me.

The church was adorned with flickering candles and fragrant flowers. The preacher stood at the altar in a long white robe. The wedding party consisted of tall, handsome ushers; a lovely maid of honor; beautiful bridesmaids; adorable flower girls; and a precious ring bearer. I was a blushing bride with a dazzling smile. I was adorned with sparkling jewelry and flawless makeup, and was wearing the traditional long white flowing gown with a long train and equally long veil. I clutched the arm of my father, who proudly escorted me down the aisle, as guests watched with anticipation. When the minister gave the rehearsed nod, my father transferred his baby girl to her new husband.

Reggie was strikingly handsome. He was taller than me even in my white spiked heels. His eyes were beaming with adoration, and I made myself believe that I was doing the right thing. Marrying Reggie was my chance to get what I always wanted — a good husband, a happy family, minus children. Nearly all of my closest girlfriends were already married, and the fairy-tale life I always dreamed about was staring me in the face, or so I thought. I couldn't walk away — this was what I dreamed about. Something inside of me kept telling me that I could make it work. That's what I wanted to believe.

When my father joined my hand with Reggie's hand, before God, family, and friends, I exhibited sheer delight at being pronounced Mrs. Reginald Hardeman. There was a passionate kiss, applause, and the ceremonious embrace of our parents. "She's all yours now, Champ," my father said to my new husband — leaving me to feel like I was property being transferred from one owner to another. At that moment, I began my Academy Award performance of pretending to be the happy bride.

Reggie, a southern-born man raised in Enfield, North Carolina, came from a tightly knit family of four sisters and two brothers. I was extremely fond of his father, a very light-skinned man who smiled a lot and had a sweet disposition — a southern gentleman. We took to each other from the moment we met. Reggie and my mother became very close; perhaps it was because his mother was deceased and my mother favored men.

There was no question that I married a hard working man who wanted to excel in life. We did not have an opportunity to go on a honeymoon because he was a newly hired DC police officer. His dream of becoming a police officer became a reality while we were engaged, and he was due to report for training at the police academy the Monday after our wedding. Police training was challenging for him, but it seemed to bring him immense satisfaction. He made new friends and worked diligently at his new profession.

Meanwhile, I thought at the very least, I was doing an outstanding job playing the role of the perfect wife — cooking, cleaning, gaining too much weight, and performing my intimate wifely duties, which I hated. To those looking from the outside in, Reggie and I were a lucky young couple who had it all. On the heels of our wedding and Reggie's entrance into the police academy, I was promoted at work to a higher level secretary. Our combined incomes allowed us to move from a one-bedroom apartment in Oxon Hill, Maryland, into a two-bedroom luxury apartment in a new development in Hillcrest Heights, Maryland, that we turned into "home beautiful" with equally luxurious furnishings. Reggie and I could easily afford pretty much whatever we wanted. We also enjoyed going on trips, shopping, buying cars, eating in upscale restaurants, and socializing regularly with family and friends.

But as good as I was at pretending, I failed miserably at loving my husband. Marriage to him was not where my heart was, and I believe he could sense it. I could not get the man I secretly loved, Stephen Graham, out of my heart and mind.

Reggie was a casual drinker when we first met. Once we were married and he became a police officer, he began to drink excessively, as did most of his friends on the force. Barely in his mid-twenties, Reggie developed severe high blood pressure, and doctors warned him that if he did not stop drinking, he would lose his life. Needless to say, he did not stop drinking. What made matters worse was that he convinced himself that I was cheating on him while he worked various shifts. His jealousy, aided by excessive alcohol consumption, caused him to explode into fits of rage that brought on physical fights.

While admittedly I was in love with another man, I did not cheat on my husband — at first. I took on additional projects to earn extra money and to fill up my alone time. Of course, my husband knew when and where I was at all times. There were occasions when I would stop by my mother's house or visit a girlfriend, because I did not want to sit in the quiet of our apartment alone. If Reggie called the apartment and I wasn't in place to answer, no matter what I said, he would accuse me of being unfaithful and a fight would ensue. I fought back to defend myself because it is not my nature to cower before anyone. I did not believe in displaying fear. I left Reggie more times than I care to count, over my mother's objection and disapproval. It was inconceivable to her that I would walk away from a man who could help provide material possessions most women would die for. She didn't consider that I contributed half of everything we had — as a matter of fact, I made the most money because I always had multiple streams of income. She was relentless in making her point that I should stay. When he gets angry, "just don't say anything" she would tell me.

Stephen and I were lovers before I met Reggie, and we maintained a distant friendship during most of my marriage to Reggie. I confided in him that I made a terrible mistake when I married Reggie, that I was miserable being married, and that a divorce was inevitable.

Less than a year into my marriage to Reggie, Stephen and I agreed to meet at a restaurant outside of the city, and when I arrived, he was waiting for me in the reception area. As I walked into the restaurant, he slowly strode toward me. My heart was thumping so loudly I was certain he could hear it. He had that kind of effect on me. He is so damn fine, I thought to myself. Through his wire-rimmed glasses, I could see him gazing at me with those dark, intense, penetrating eyes, as if he was looking right into my very soul. There was plenty for him to gaze at. Existing in an unhappy and abusive marriage, I comforted myself with food and went from a sexy, medium-sized young woman, to a married, overweight, unhappy mess. We politely embraced, made small talk, and waited to be seated. Strangely, the moment we were seated at our table and began chatting about old times, that all-too-familiar chemistry between us emerged. Actually, the connection we shared was as strong as ever.

During our marriage, I left Reggie at least four times. Each time I left him, I would eventually return to his unrelenting accusations and abuse. Everything would be fine for a while, but the abuse would start again every time. Each time I returned to him, I did so with the honest intention of making my marriage work. Our two-bedroom luxury apartment became a revolving door, with me moving in and out so often the rental agent warned that if another move occurred, she would be forced to terminate our lease. I grew more than weary of Reggie's accusations, drinking, fighting, battering, and intimidation. One night when he came home after drinking with the boys, an altercation started with his usual accusations. At that point, I knew it was over. I was done. I was preparing to leave with the thought of coming back later for the rest of my things. Before I knew what was happening, Reggie had smacked me against the side of my head. This time, I didn't fight back. I didn't say a word. To this day I don't know why, but I picked up a new bottle of nail polish and simply left the apartment. I never looked back. He called my mother, pleading with her to talk to me. "He loves you," my mother said, hoping to help his cause. "Ain't nothing else out here." Only this time there was nothing my mother or my husband could say that would entice me to consider returning to a marriage that should have never happened in the first place.

On December 20, 1973, a little more than a year after my wedding day, I was granted an absolute divorce from Reggie. (He died on my birthday, April 1, 2008.)

Now, with this sad ordeal behind me, I vowed to get it right the next time. I was still determined to have my happy family, because this time I would love the man I would marry. I knew exactly who I loved — the man I should have waited to marry. The man I was in love with when I married Reggie. The man, who in spite of his fear of commitment and problems with fidelity, must have known in his heart that we were meant to be together. After all, now we were both single and available, and that was a good sign for me. So, I went after the man I believed I deserved.

CHAPTER 15
HUSBAND NUMBER TWO

Stephen Graham was husband number two — the man I was in love with two weeks after we met, the man I loved when I married Reginald Hardeman, the man I will always respect. Stephen was the one I was certain would give me my happy family if I could convince him to settle down with me. Getting him to the altar proved to be no easy task, because he was no more interested in making a commitment to me than before I married Reggie. He was quiet, reserved, and had a soft voice. He was extremely handsome and always immaculately groomed — six-feet, four inches tall, with a reddish-brown complexion, and a neatly trimmed mustache. Because he was the only male in his tight-knit family of two sisters and his mother, Stephen was cherished, catered to, protected, and given whatever he wanted. He was the consummate ladies' man and relished every minute of it. Women flocked to him like bees to honey, all for his choosing. But I did not allow his womanizing to discourage me from my goal of being the only woman in his life. I pursued him with all the gusto I had. I wanted to make this dream come alive — to become his wife.

After I left Reggie, I moved into a high-rise apartment in Southwest DC that was a popular residence for young black professionals. I treasured my new beginning — new apartment, new furniture, new car, new life — but I did not like being alone.

It was not long before Stephen began visiting me at my new apartment. The first time he visited me after the divorce, I was caught completely off guard. I was ridiculously nervous, like an anxious teenager preparing for her first date. When he telephoned to tell me that he was on his way to my apartment, I paced the floor, peeping out the balcony window watching for his car. The moment I saw him pull into the parking lot, my heart began to pound like a drum. I tried to compose myself as best I could, while anxiously awaiting his knock on my door. Greeting him with a warm smile, I gave him a quick tour of the apartment, proud of my interior-design skills. We made ourselves comfortable on the black leather sofa in the living room and talked, enjoyed cocktails, and listened to soft music. Of course, he stayed overnight, a night that was sheer magic. Our lovemaking, like always, was slow and filled with ecstasy, a clear sign to me that Stephen and I were meant to be together.

We saw each other as often as possible, and always on the weekends. Stephen was a photographer with a local university and had a passion for art. I took on more responsibility at work with higher pay. My position required occasional travel, and during those times, I missed him terribly. Our free time was spent together and our relationship finally became serious. Things were finally going as planned. While we enjoyed each other, we were quite different. I was an extrovert and Stephen was, for the most part, an introvert. For the longest time, I thought he couldn't dance, but while playing music one night at the apartment, we danced together for the first time. Surprisingly, he was a good hand-dancer — graceful, easy to follow, and light on his feet. He was smooth and rhythmic, leaving me to wonder why he refused to dance in public. But what mattered to me most was making him happy. I did not hold back how I felt about him. Whenever we were together, our world mirrored the lives of characters in romance novels.

Stephen seemed happy and I was ecstatic — until he began not showing up as promised and breaking dates. I was frantic that our relationship was eroding and I did not know why. We began to argue frequently. I threatened to call off the relationship many times but never did. Finally, I demanded to know where I stood in his life.

Eventually, I found out exactly where I stood, and that there was a reason for his mysterious behavior. On a bright summer Sunday morning in June 1974, I learned the truth, and was dumbfounded for not having seen the clues.

The night before, we had made a date, agreeing to meet at my apartment, but nothing special had been planned. I got dressed, put on my makeup, and waited for my man. It was getting late and Stephen hadn't arrived and hadn't called. I lay across the bed feeling uncomfortable about his recent behavior, but managed to fall into a restless sleep. The next morning, I awoke, realized that he had stood me up again, and was livid. I walked out onto the balcony to clear my head. As I looked out on the parking lot, I noticed a familiar-looking brown sedan, which I was certain belonged to Connor Middleton, Stephen's very close friend. Hoping that I was wrong, I telephoned Connor's home. His wife, Kathleen, answered the phone.

"Kathleen," I said, hesitantly.

"Nesa," she responded. "Hi, baby, what's up?"

"Is Connor's car at your house?"

"Hold on, let me check."

I waited, nervous, scared, and hoping that Connor's car was there.

"No, Connor's car isn't here," Kathleen said, "But Stephen's car is out front. They must have switched cars for some reason."

"Is Connor at home now?" I asked.

"Yes," she replied. "He's sleeping."

"Connor's car is in my parking lot," I said, "and I'm going to get to the bottom of what's going on." I thanked Kathleen and hung up the phone. I was beyond angry. I dashed out of the apartment and hurriedly took the elevator down to the lobby. At that time, I didn't know where Stephen was or whom he was with, but I was going to find out. My heart racing, I ran through the parking lot, jumped into my car, and drove up to Connor's brown sedan, which was parked with the front wheels facing the curb. I drove my car behind Connor's vehicle, touching the bumper, sandwiching the car between the curb and my car. I went back up to my apartment balcony to keep a close watch for Stephen. Well into the afternoon, I saw him stroll out of the building heading toward Connor's car. He froze in his footsteps the second he realized that it was my car blocking Connor's car. The man who I believed was destined to be my second husband was flat busted. I stormed out of my apartment to confront him.

"Why?" I angrily asked.

"I guess I'm just a dog," Stephen casually responded.

I was crushed. It was bad enough that he remained so cool and calm in the middle of this painful ordeal, but it got worse. Stephen wasn't just having a one-night fling. While I had been waiting for Stephen to spend time with me, he was an elevator ride away, just a few floors above my apartment, having an ongoing relationship with another woman — a woman I had seen on numerous occasions and with whom I had exchanged polite greetings. Stephen even had the audacity to tell me that she knew about me. Yet, I knew nothing about her.

"Don't ever call me again," I hissed. I got into my car, backed away from Connor's car, parked near the apartment entrance, and disappeared into the building. I felt humiliated, like I was dying inside. I did not want to believe what had just happened, what I had just heard, what I had just seen with my own eyes.

Like the typical guilty man, Stephen started with the phone calls, calmly pleading his case, apologizing profusely, imploring me to see him, to talk with him so that we could "work things out." I refused to see him. Eventually, Stephen gave up trying to patch things up, and we went our separate ways.

Our separation, however, lasted all of three months. I missed Stephen terribly. Giving in to my feelings, I called him from work. I was honest, telling him how much I missed him and that I wanted to see him. We talked about what happened and agreed to resume our relationship — this time, a monogamous one. Things were different this time around as we were serious about making our relationship work. He spent all of his free time with me, socializing with friends, attending family functions, going for walks in Rock Creek Park, where he enjoyed taking photos of the surrounding nature and me. Yes, we were finally, unmistakably a couple. I loved him with every ounce of my being, and was willing to do whatever it took to make it last. Nothing was more important to me than being with him.

On New Year's Eve 1973, Stephen and I returned to my apartment from a fun evening with friends. We were both happy and in our usual lusty mood. I was full of libations, giddy, and careless, neglecting to use my diaphragm. The following month, I missed my menstrual cycle.

"I just can't be pregnant," I said to myself.

"You're pregnant," the doctor said.

I wasn't sure what to do or how to feel. Having children was nowhere on my "to do" list; but since it was Stephen's child, I saw a slight ray of sunlight in my predicament — a good husband and father. Leaving the doctor's office, I nervously telephoned Stephen from a pay phone. When he answered, I went straight to the point. "Stephen, I just came from the doctor. I'm pregnant."

Surprisingly, a man who had dodged making a commitment of any kind was happy to learn that he was going to be a father. He matter-of-factly said, "Well, I will move in with you." I told him we would need a larger place and he agreed. Together we found a spacious two-bedroom apartment in Silver Spring, Maryland. Stephen was every bit the proud expectant father and used his skills as a professional photographer to capture my growing body throughout my pregnancy.

For seven months of my pregnancy, I was sicker than sick with severe nausea, and was swollen from head to toe. The edema was so extreme that when I washed my face, the pores on my nose would bleed. My breasts were extremely full and painful, so much so that I would go into the bathroom at work and put ice packs on them to ease the throbbing pain. While driving home from work, I would vomit in the car from the smell of the car and bus exhaust fumes.

I couldn't wait to have the baby, and resolved that this would be my only pregnancy. On October 16, 1974, I gave birth to a nine-pound, two-ounce baby boy. We named him Richard Duncan Graham. I thanked God for giving us a healthy boy, and was thankful that he would not suffer what I went through. I embraced Stephen's energy as a new father. Baby Richard was our joy. He was a happy, fat, jolly baby with kissable chubby cheeks and full, pouting lips. Though children had never been a part of my dream, I realized that I was just a step away from having my happy family — a good husband and a son we both absolutely adored. Without a doubt, I knew that whatever happened, Stephen would be there for his son because he grew up without his father. He often expressed his anger and disappointment because his father had never been in his life, and he was adamant that he would always be in his son's life.

In December 1974, two months after our baby was born, Stephen and I were married in a quiet, intimate, early-evening ceremony witnessed by a few close relatives at a Catholic church in Northwest DC.

We made an effort to settle into our marriage, but there was little time to enjoy wedded bliss. Although I had six weeks of maternity leave after Richard was born, taking care of him was challenging. He was irritable with colic until we discovered he was allergic to milk. There were many nights when we barely got any sleep. During many early mornings, I felt so alone — no one else could possibly be up with a colicky, crying baby at four o'clock in the morning except me, I thought. There were nights when I cried as much as the baby.

After six weeks in the role of wife, mother, nurse, housekeeper, and cook, I eagerly returned to work with new vigor and an insatiable thirst for personal growth. I shared my professional aspirations with my husband; however, Stephen made it unmistakably clear that he was completely satisfied with life as it was. He loved his son, his profession as a photographer, and me. And even though the photography profession barely paid the bills, it was important to me that my husband was happy.

But I still became disillusioned, and my family was no help. My mother had disliked Stephen from the beginning, viewing him as conceited and arrogant. A rumor that I was financially supporting my husband because he thought he was "too good" to work quickly reached the eager ears of every family member. It was not an issue for me that he did not make mega bucks; but I wanted more — more education, more income, more challenges, more everything.

At twenty-four, while holding down a full-time job at the association where I had worked since graduating from high school, I began to realize the importance of higher education and I looked for ways to reach my goal. I saw women — including black women — holding professional positions. I worked as a high-level secretary for Dr. Sharon McCune, who encouraged me to further my education. As a manager for the women's program, she was smart, confident, and strong. She was a white woman who mentored me and introduced me to feminist ideology, which, at that time, was foreign to me, but ultimately helped shape who I am today.

I embraced the notion of "women's rights" and began to believe that higher education would significantly benefit my family. Stephen maintained his calm and easygoing life as a photographer. He also liked the nicer things in life, but was not the aggressive type to work fourteen hours a day in a corporate setting. His world did not revolve around a job. He was concerned about our finances, but not to the point of becoming stressed over it. I was always worried about finances and, over time became frustrated with his laid-back demeanor.

My aggressive nature did not intimidate him; rather, he seemed to admire it. Too immature to work out our differences or explore ways to compromise, we both began to look outside our marriage for support, validation, and comfort. Stephen began having affairs, and I also had a brief affair, further damaging our already fragile marriage.

Richard was two years old when Stephen and I separated; and three years after pledging my life to the man that I loved for years, I signed divorce papers again. Unlike the relief I felt after my first divorce, this divorce was unimaginably painful.

Stephen and I agreed to put aside our feelings of anger and hurt and focus on what was in the best interest of our son. After the divorce, Richard attended a parochial school near my mother's home for two years, and lived with her during the week. Either Stephen or I picked him up on weekends and holidays. When taking care of a rambunctious child became too much for my then fifty-eight-year-old mother, Stephen and I decided that Richard would live with him. He wanted to take on a more proactive role in his son's life. He stressed how important it was for him to have a strong male influence, and said that he could guide him into manhood. I agreed. My childhood was damaged to the point I was afraid to raise my own son; afraid I did not know how to be a good mother. I honestly believed that it was better for Richard to live with his father and for me to have him on weekends.

My son was fortunate and blessed with not just a father, but a wonderful man who wanted to be a daddy. Despite our failed marriage, I had complete confidence that Stephen and I would raise our son to be a good man with strong principles. I understood that Richard needed from his father the important elements of a close-knit family, with minimal dysfunction, which I could not provide. My family never had the good fortune to really get to know my son, but knowing that Richard was with Stephen and his family, I knew I did not have to worry about my son being abused — physically, verbally, emotionally, sexually, or psychologically. My son would be safe and well-cared-for, and of course I would always do my part. I often wonder if this is how my mother might have felt when she left me in the care of Aunt Constance.

* * *

Stephen raised our son to be a good and strong man. Based on my childhood experiences, I believed I could not do the job as well as his father. Raising Richard also pushed Stephen to become a more responsible person because his son was his number one priority. He taught our son lessons the way only a father could – respect, responsibility, consciousness, a sense of community, and a love of learning. Richard also learned that knowledge is power—that's the "me" in him. But most importantly, Stephen taught our son to respect his mother and women in general. For that, I will be forever grateful to Stephen Graham.

My son and I share a healthy mother-son bond. We talk about everything. There isn't much Richard doesn't know about me. There isn't a question he has asked that I haven't answered honestly, even if it hurts. He knows how much I love him. We enjoy our time together, and he knows that being raised by his father was a decision I have never regretted.

Though Richard spends most holidays with his paternal side of the family, he visits me frequently and telephones often and there are times that he alternates holidays to spend with me. Now that I have health issues, he arranges his already challenging schedule to spend even more time with me. Although divorced, Stephen and I have always treated each other with respect and compassion from the time of Richard's birth to the present. I am an admiring witness to the character of my son, who is now a father. Fruits of his parents' labor are present as I watch him parent my granddaughter — a miniature Nesa Chappelle and a handful to say the least. I am aware that, where she is concerned, I have my work cut out for me. At six years old, my granddaughter is a little genius. I have already begun giving her stern but unconditional love and stimulating, age-appropriate conversations. Because of my experience at a young age with sexual abuse, I talk to her about inappropriate touching and what to do and whom to tell immediately if it should occur. My granddaughter and I (NaNa, as she calls me) have these serious talks often. It is important to me that she understands that she has absolutely no reason to be frightened or ashamed to come to her parents or to me about anything for any reason. There are times when Richard becomes impatient with me because of the perceived preoccupation that I have about children and all forms of abuse. I will not apologize for what I know because it happened to me and it happens to children entirely too often. Molestation is devastating to children and can have a negative impact on them for the rest of their lives.

My granddaughter is precious to all of us. We share fond memories through shared stories and photos of Richard as a baby and now of our Miss Raya — taken with love by Grandpa Stephen. I am so very proud of my son. I admire the way he lives life on his terms and I am forever thankful that his father devoted his life to ensuring that our son became a responsible man.

When my marriage to Stephen ended, I never imagined that I would hear myself say these words: "The father of my son will always hold a special place in my heart." I've often told Stephen, "I could not have chosen a better man as a father for my son than you." At this writing, there are no words to describe just how much I appreciate and respect him. All I can say is that he will forever be favorably etched in my heart.

CHAPTER 16
HUSBAND NUMBER THREE

TSUNAMI
*Terror comes all of a sudden without enough time to
plan how to get to high ground to avoid death by
drowning.*
*There's a calm and all of a sudden for the smallest little
thing, all hell breaks loose. He's in his other self now —
that other thing – it has become active. You didn't see it
coming so you couldn't prepare to make your exit in time
— you're caught up in the walls of fury. Death by
drowning is imminent.*

— Nesa Chappelle, Ph.D.

My quest for more — career challenges, education, financial sta-
bility — did not subside. I continued to work unbelievably long
hours. In 1976, I was studying for an undergraduate degree
with heavy course loads at night and caring for my son on weekends.

There was very little time for a social life, except for an occasional
outing for cocktails with friends. On one of those outings, I met Willie
Frye, another Washington, DC, police officer. He was tall, dark, and
handsome, and involved with a woman he had been seeing for quite
some time. He was honest, funny, and very sociable, and we hung out
together for a very brief period.

During our short friendship, Willie and I found the time to play match-
maker. We introduced Janice, my lifelong friend and confidante, and Taylor, Willie's friend, and an interesting relationship developed between

them. One autumn evening, Taylor and Janice asked me to join them to visit Willie and other friends at his mother's home in DC.

When we arrived, a small group of people were exchanging small talk. Willie and Taylor exchanged pleasantries while Janice and I made ourselves comfortable in the small living room. Shortly after taking a seat on the sofa, I noticed a man closely resembling the singer Teddy Pendergrass sitting in an oversized chair, off from the others, quietly watching television. "How y'all doing this evening?" he asked, smiling, showing off a set of pearly white teeth that glistened against his dark-chocolate, smooth, flawless skin. He had a coal-black beard, the build of Adonis, and was the sexiest man I had ever laid eyes on.

"Fine," Janice and I said. I displayed a cordial smile, without revealing that he had captured my interest.

"I'm Derrick," he said.

"I'm Nesa," I said.

"I'm Janice," my friend replied.

Charming, witty, with a great sense of humor, and fine as hell, Derrick engaged us in what I thought was a rather interesting conversation. Mid-evening quickly turned to late evening. Janice beckoned, saying that she and Taylor were preparing to leave. Because it had become dark outside, I also decided to leave, not wanting to be out alone too late.

"I'll walk you out," Derrick said as he escorted me to my red Corvette with my name on the tags. Janice and Taylor said goodnight and sped off in Taylor's car while Derrick and I stood chatting next to my car. As I was about to leave, he asked for my telephone number. By then, I had found out that the man I had spent the majority of the evening talking to was not just another guest. He was Willie Frye's baby brother.

Although Willie and I were never a couple, I told Derrick that in the previous year, Willie and I had hung out together briefly. Derrick shrugged it off in a manner that indicated that my relationship with his brother was not important to him.

We exchanged telephone numbers, and I was not the least bit surprised when he called the very next day. It was clear during our conversation that we wanted to see each other again, and we began to see each other periodically. Of course, I was careful not to get too emotionally attached to a man whose fiancée, in a matter of months, would give birth to his child.

One morning, as I was preparing to leave for work, Derrick telephoned me with heartbreaking news — their baby was stillborn. Loving my son with all of my heart, I could only imagine the pain Derrick and his fiancée were experiencing over their loss. Though Derrick and I never discussed his fiancée in-depth, I was genuinely sad for them both. I urged Derrick to take time to grieve, and I resolved to bow out of his life. But in a few weeks, Derrick called and said his relationship with his fiancée was over. Shocked, I asked what happened, but he did not want to talk about it. Instead, he asked if he could see me.

Shortly thereafter, we began dating frequently, but I did not expect a serious relationship to develop between us, and I certainly never saw another marriage on the horizon.

Snow was falling by the buckets on a cold wintry night in the DC metropolitan area, and residents were urged to stay indoors because the roads were extremely hazardous. When Derrick telephoned to ask if he could come over, I repeated the warning to stay off the roads, but he insisted that he would be fine. The snow was already close to four inches deep, but he was determined to get to my apartment. Three hours later, I heard his big work truck rumbling in front of my apartment building. I peeped out of my window and saw this gorgeous hunk of a man — who was determined to weather the storm to be with me — parking his truck. Minutes later he was knocking on my door.

That night a romance blossomed that sealed our relationship, and we became inseparable. I was completely caught off guard and my feelings for Derrick grew. I never thought I would feel this way about anyone after Stephen. I thought we were right for each other. Derrick was an extrovert who delighted in socializing, dancing, telling jokes, and having fun, all of which brought new energy into my dull, lonely, insecure, needy life. I loved to cook and entertain friends, so we complemented each other very well on that level. Our friends and families enjoyed being in our company because Derrick made sure everyone had a great time

— always more than enough food and liquor and never a dull moment. Still, I was a hard worker with a plethora of untapped goals and ambitions. Derrick was also a hard worker with a strong work ethic, something I attributed to his being born and raised in the mountains of Lexington, Kentucky. He was the ultimate provider with an uncanny ability for finding ways to double, sometimes triple, the income he earned driving a truck for a small company in Rockville, Maryland. Derrick saw to it that I got whatever I wanted and more. We were also, thankfully, sexually compatible, which was rare for me in relationships. Initially Derrick was gentle, loving, and kind, and I allowed myself to love again.

I just knew I hit the jackpot with Derrick. What more could I ask for in a man? I liked everything about him — his masculinity, good looks, fun-loving ways, sex, his ability to provide for our comfortable living, and importantly, his positive interaction with my son.

For the first time since my marriage to Stephen, I was confident that I had finally gotten it right — I had found my soul mate.

I believed that with a man like Derrick by my side, we could enjoy each other more fully living together rather than separately. In October 1978, Derrick moved into my two-bedroom apartment and within a few months, problems began to surface. The sad truth is I was in denial about Derrick's heavy drinking, not allowing myself to think "alcoholic" again.

After a while, living with him was like living with Dr. Jekyll and Mr. Hyde. When Derrick was not drinking, he was quiet, sweet, and reserved. When he was drinking, the change was instantaneous. He became a hilarious extrovert, but he also became irrational and agitated, exhibiting signs of jealousy and insecurity, such as criticizing my clothing — "dress too tight," "blouse too low." One New Year's Eve, a simple disagreement erupted into a heated argument and Derrick stormed out of the apartment in a huff, not returning until the next evening. I was furious! As soon as he opened the door, I was in his face demanding to know where he had been all night, and on New Year's Eve at that. He said he had gone to a buddy's house, had too much to drink, and fell asleep. I didn't believe a word of it and accused him of lying. We began to exchange shouts and screams. His rage erupted into a physical assault. I was extremely angry

Husband Number Three

and we went blow for blow. I don't know to this day where I got the strength to hang in there with him, but I did. His size and strength didn't mean a thing to me at that time. When he slapped me, I socked him back. He punched me. I punched and kicked him back. I thought that if one of us went out on a stretcher that night, so be it.

Derrick must have thought I was losing my mind, because he moved away from me and called Jerome, his oldest brother, who was also a DC police officer, and another married player. "I'm going to kill this girl if you don't come get her," he said. I reminded him he was in my apartment and he was the one who was leaving. Jerome must have broken every speed limit in Maryland because he was banging on the apartment door in record time. Jerome spoke privately with Derrick and then with me until we both calmed down. Once Jerome left, Derrick began making attempts to assure me that no other woman was involved. Of course, I knew he was lying and he knew that I knew he was lying.

Again, instead of acting on the truth and heeding the warning signs, I accepted his lies and continued the sick behavior pattern that I learned from the lonely and abused women in my family. All men cheat. As long as he comes home to you and pay the bills, don't worry about it, they would say.

In December 1978, I earned my bachelor of science degree in education with a concentration in Spanish and business education, and I assumed that I would be promoted from the administrative pool to a professional rank. I wanted very much to grow at the organization with people who had practically become family to me for the past nine years, but for some reason, I was not provided the opportunity to move into a professional position. Although the organization was advancing public education, it was not progressive enough to advance the careers of support staff, even after investing time and money in their education. After being rejected numerous times for a promotion, I made the difficult and scary decision to leave the organization to pursue my master's degree and obtain a professional position elsewhere.

I secured a position at the DC Board of Education as a bilingual education assistant. Within a year, I was offered a wonderful opportunity to serve as the liaison between the DC Public Schools and SER (Service,

Employment, and Redevelopment and Spanish for "to be") — Jobs For Progress, a nonprofit Hispanic organization responsible for developing the first multicultural high school in Washington, DC. In this position, I was responsible for recruiting and certifying bilingual and English-as-a-second-language teachers, assisting the director with public relations and media campaigns, and ensuring that the multicultural high school complied with the policies and procedures established by the DC Board of Education.

My prior experience with the board, my status as a certified bilingual high school teacher, and my tireless ambition for excellence made me a natural fit for the position. The director of the new high school, a young Hispanic woman, provided the environment and support that enabled me to succeed in my first highly visible professional position. I was required to attend meetings conducted in Spanish, with various dialects, which forced me to immerse myself in the Hispanic community, where I received unbelievably wonderful support. Being recognized and accepted by colleagues and the community as a qualified professional, capable of handling and being accountable for important responsibilities, was exhilarating, and boosted my confidence. My college education finally paid off. Unfortunately, the organization was not the one from which I planned to retire.

On a memorable Saturday evening, instead of entertaining at home, which we did routinely, Derrick and I visited Sonny and Rita Brown, a couple with whom we often spent time. As soon as we entered their home, Josh, their eleven-year-old son, exclaimed, "Dag, Derrick, every time I see you, you're with a different lady!" Derrick ignored the remark and struck up a conversation with Sonny as if he hadn't heard a word Josh said. I already knew Derrick was a cheat, but to learn from Josh's statement that he was having numerous affairs with different women and bringing them around people who knew me was too much. When we returned to the apartment that evening, I demanded to know why he would take other women to the same places he took me. A heated argument ensued, and Derrick ranted, raved, and stormed out of the house as though he was the wronged person. He drove to Willie's home, the place where he, his brother James, and his other married friends could safely rendezvous with their lovers.

I waited up nearly all night to continue my confrontation with Derrick. He didn't come home. The next day, I repeatedly called Willie's house from my office, but no one answered. During my lunch hour, I drove to Willie's house and Derrick's blue van was parked on the street. I pulled up behind it, got out of my car, and pounded on the door. No one answered, so I left in a huff. A week, if not more, passed and I hadn't seen or heard a word from the man who said he "loved" me. Again, on a sunny afternoon, during my lunch break, I left my office and drove to Willie's house. No one answered, but Derrick's van was again parked in front of the house. This time, I opened the mail slot of the door and shouted, "I want your things out of my house!" No one responded, and I did not hear a sound. Even though I could not see anyone as I peeped through the mail slot, my gut told me that Derrick was in there, and probably with his lover. I decided not to make a scene, and got in my car and left. I felt like such a fool — like a desperate idiot, humiliated by a man once again.

Later that evening, I arrived home from work, my emotions still raw. The telephone rang. It was Derrick. He said he wanted to talk and asked if I would pick him up from Willie's home. Although I could not fathom why he wanted me to pick him up, I agreed because I wanted to hear what he had to say. When I arrived at Willie's house, I blew the horn once and Derrick emerged from his brother's house in a pair of jeans, an unbuttoned shirt exposing his sexy, hairy, muscular chest. He got into my car. "You want to go get something to eat?" he asked, as if nothing ever happened. I didn't respond. Like a robot, I drove to a nearby McDonald's, parked the car, and we went inside. I took a seat at the table across from Derrick.

"Why?" I asked.

"Because you pissed me off," he said, looking me straight in the eye as if I was to blame. It is always somebody else's fault, I would learn.

"Where did you meet her?" I asked, inquiring about his lover.

"That time I went to New Jersey," he responded, nonchalantly. "She doesn't mean anything to me," he continued.

Derrick began apologizing, making empty promises, and pleading with me to believe that "it would never happen again." I knew better, but I clung to the dysfunctional relationship anyway. In my mind, all men cheated.

Given my experience with men at that time, I did not have to look far to see clearly what lay ahead for me. I was conscious of the problematic life I would have if I remained with Derrick. That is why it is important that I state plainly, leaving no room for doubt, that I am not pointing the finger of blame at anyone but myself. I made the decision to stay with Derrick even though I had similar problems before. I take full responsibility for each of my poor choices when it came to relationships with men. Derrick displayed his jealous, controlling, and abusive tendencies while we were dating and after we moved in together.

In April 1979, Derrick and I moved into a beautiful, newly built townhouse in the Adams Morgan area of Washington, DC, closer to my place of employment. It was pure hell studying for a master's degree, working full time, and putting up with Derrick's foolishness. It was more than apparent that my determination for higher education was intimidating to him. But his tirades did not stop my pursuit of the graduate degree. In May 1980, I received my master of education degree from George Mason University in Fairfax, Virginia. I cannot describe the feeling of accomplishment the day I received the degree. I was happy to have Derrick and my father and mother in the audience to witness my triumph. I had never seen my father look so proud. He would not have missed seeing me receive a graduate degree for anything in this world. I was making history in the family. Education was definitely on the top of his "wish I had" list, and he lived vicariously through my accomplishments.

Derrick never mustered up any excitement or exhibited any joy over my receiving a master's degree. Instead, he was uneasy, and his jealousy and need to control intensified. And afterward, I had the audacity to mention pursuing a Ph.D.

While studying for my bachelor's and master's degrees, I endured Derrick's numerous drunken, jealous, insecure fits of rage. I wanted desperately to do whatever was necessary to avoid enduring that same hell again. So, not long after receiving my master's degree, I began talking to Derrick about my wish to further my education. My hope was to warm him up to the idea before I actually enrolled in a doctoral program. When Derrick was free of alcohol, he seemed receptive to the notion, but if he had been drinking, he would fly off the handle, yelling and ranting. "All you want to do is copy off of Yvonne. You only want your Ph.D. 'cause she got hers! You always got to be better than everybody else, don't you?" I tried in every way I knew to convince Derrick that my desire for a Ph.D. had nothing to do with competing with his sister-in-law, Yvonne, or trying to be an elitist.

On a stifling hot day in August 1981, Derrick and I were married at a trendy lounge in Washington, with more than fifty guests. I was dressed in an elegant, beige floor-length dress with a matching wide-brim hat that covered stylish braids tightly pulled into a bun at the nape of my neck. As I slowly emerged down a set of spiral steps holding a bouquet of silk flowers, Derrick, handsome and immaculately dressed in a black suit, matching tie and shoes, and a beige shirt, stood waiting at the bottom of the staircase to escort me to the platform where everyone could see and hear us. Before God, we pledged our love, loyalty, and commitment to one another until death us do part. As the music began to softly play, he took me in his arms, kissed me tenderly, and we had our first dance as man and wife to Larry Graham's "Just Be My Lady."

The wedding ceremony began and ended like a fairytale. Two of my girlfriends drove from Chicago to attend the wedding. Derrick and I were to begin our married life in a luxurious honeymoon suite at an upscale Washington hotel. But, as fate would have it, he got drunk on our wedding night. Instead, we spent our honeymoon at Willie's untidy bachelor's pad, because we had reservations elsewhere and our house was full of overnight guests who attended the wedding. I lay there beside my new husband in a state of utter disgust and disbelief that this was actually happening to me. I cried the entire night while the drunk I married was oblivious to everything. The next morning, Derrick pretended he did not understand what the big deal was that we did not stay in the honeymoon suite, and was totally insensitive to my disappointment. I never forgot that night.

The beginning of our first year as husband and wife was uneventful. Surprisingly, I found myself eagerly making plans for Derrick's two daughters from previous relationships and my son to spend time together as siblings. Our first Christmas was wonderful. On Christmas Eve, my son and one of Derrick's daughters, who was visiting us, woke up in the wee hours of the morning, crept quietly downstairs, and opened all of the gifts — theirs and everybody else's. When Derrick and I came downstairs and discovered the mess they had made, we laughed until we cried. As kids, it was only natural for them to think that all of the gifts belonged to them. We called our friends to join in our laughter over what our children had done. That Christmas we exchanged unwrapped gifts; in that precious moment, I was happy.

Toward the end of our first year of marriage, there had been physical fights, and I left him numerous times, only to return home. I pleaded with him to get help for his drinking. I wanted to believe that, if he could get help for his alcohol addiction, our marriage might survive. I was willing to go to counseling with him and do whatever it took to help him get well. I did not want to lose my husband or my marriage. When he refused to seek help, I asked him, "What is more important, liquor or our marriage?"

"Hennessey is my wife!" he quickly snapped.

From that day forward, I resigned myself to what I should expect the second my husband poured the first glass of "Ms. Hennessey," his real wife. Sometimes it was as if all it took was for Derrick to smell "Ms. Hennessey," and I was in for physical and verbal abuse. It did not matter that I maintained an immaculate house, prepared home-cooked meals, entertained guests and family at his whim, or performed my wifely duties; I absolutely could not compete with the love of his life — "Ms. Hennessey." I wanted more than words can describe to keep my marriage intact. I just could not fathom another failure. Then fate stepped in —again.

I was home alone on a lovely spring evening, when I decided to visit Jasmine Crenshaw, a friend and neighbor who lived around the corner from our house. When Derrick got home from work to find me not at home, he went in search of me. Jasmine answered a knock at her door, and I heard her invite Derrick inside.

"Naw," he said. "I just came for Nesa." Up until that time, my day had gone well. My visits with Jasmine always put me in good spirits, but as soon as I approached the door and caught a glimpse of the look on his face, I knew how the day would end.

"Let's go," Derrick said, extremely agitated.

To prevent any confrontation in Jasmine's home, I left without hesitation. I had barely gotten both feet on the ground outside when Derrick unleashed his uncontrollable rage. He beat me all the way home — the longest quarter of a Washington, DC, block I had traveled in my life. Men, women, and children stood across the street, watching, but not one person, that I could see, offered to lift a finger to help me.

I did everything I could to protect myself from his blows. I looked for something to grab to hit him with, but there was nothing. This was one time I knew better than to even try to fight back, because on this day, Derrick's abuse was like nothing I had ever experienced before. He was relentless — pummeling me with his fists, kicking me, while hurling vicious, ugly words. I sincerely thought that this time he was going to kill me, and I had no idea why he was hitting me — I never knew. He beat me up the cement steps leading to the front door of our townhouse, knocked me into the foyer, and actually kicked me up the stairs to the second floor where he shoved me into the bathroom, located in the back of the house, and locked the door. I fell to the floor sobbing, bleeding, with my body pulsating with pain. I don't know how much time had passed when I heard a knock at the front door.

"Police! Open up!"

"Thank God," I moaned. Someone had lifted a finger to help. Someone had called the police.

"Police! Open up!"

Derrick wouldn't answer the door and I later learned why. His brother, a DC police officer, apparently told Derrick that, according to police policy, officers of the law, without tangible evidence of a life-or-death situation, could not forcefully enter a private home. I struggled to stand up and screamed for help at the top of my lungs. I could hear the police talking outside, but they could not hear me screaming from the back of the house. After a while, the officers left, not knowing whether I needed medical attention or whether I was dead or alive. I slumped on the bathroom floor in despair. That night, the bathtub was my bed.

The next morning, I heard the lock on the bathroom door click. Derrick slithered in, hung over as usual, supposedly remorseful, apologizing profusely. "Why?" I asked him as he came into the bathroom; as if I thought I was going to get the truth or that there was any rational reason for his action. All Derrick would say was that he was sorry and that it would never happen again. I heard those words many times before!

I still didn't leave him. I knew it would happen again as long as Derrick refused to get help for his alcohol addiction. I just could not fathom another failed marriage, and was willing to fight, to compromise, to turn a blind eye a hundred times, to pray to God nonstop, whatever it took to prevent another failed marriage and another divorce. I even persuaded Derrick to talk with my minister about our marriage. He attended one session and refused to go back. Nothing changed, because he clung to "Ms. Hennessey" over our marriage.

One cold, rainy night, Derrick attacked me for the last time. I left our townhouse in my bare feet and went to a friend's house with nothing on but my housecoat and undergarments. Just tired, I finally accepted the fact that I could not win. I did not step foot again in the house I shared with Derrick except to get belongings. As I was moving out of my beautiful townhouse, I saw Derrick drive slowly by. He didn't stop — he just looked. I was no longer afraid. I finally had enough and made a promise that day that no man would ever force me to give up my home or anything else that I worked for ever again. I meant those words from the very depth of my soul.

Immediately, I filed for divorce. My marriage to Derrick was over — my third failure. It hurt like hell, but I was able to slowly move on with the knowledge that I gave the marriage all I had.

Now that I was free from another abuser, this was the perfect opportunity for me to choose being alone rather than ending up with the wrong man again.

Husband Number Three

My educational goals for the moment were achieved and I moved full-speed ahead down the road to conquer my next goal — to become a successful entrepreneur. This road, and the next whirlwind season of my life, proved to be rough, but for different reasons.

CHAPTER 17

A FRIEND INDEED

A fter leaving Derrick, I decided to leave DC Public Schools as well when another opportunity grabbed my interest — to work for a nonprofit social service organization dedicated to assisting runaway youth. My job required extensive travel, and the getaways allowed me time to mourn the loss of my third marriage. During one of my frequent trips, I attended a conference in Tampa, Florida, where I met Darryl Barrow, a tall, dark-brown-skinned man with a charming smile and a medium-sized Afro. He was an organizer and activist for a social service organization in San Diego, California. Following a particularly grueling work session, Darryl joined me and a few other conference attendees with whom we had bonded to spend a well-deserved night out exploring the city of Tampa. We enjoyed great cuisine, danced at a "sizzling hot" nightclub, and toasted the evening with a few stiff cocktails. Darryl was interesting — an African American professional man who was committed to working for social justice.

During our short time together at the conference, Darryl and I became inseparable. He was different from the men I knew and married. We knew our time together was limited, and wished we had more time to get to know each other better — but we didn't.

At the conclusion of the conference, I said my good-byes to my new-found friends, but Darryl asked to share a cab with me to the airport. My flight was scheduled to leave first so we spent time chatting while I waited to board. When the flight was announced for boarding, he asked if he could contact me. I will not deny that a strong chemistry had developed between us during our first night out. Darryl was in a relationship with a woman in California, and I told him that I was recently divorced.

Darryl was a boost to my feminine ego, damaged by years of living with Derrick's abuse. He was something new for me — the first professional man I had ever dated. I reveled in this new experience even after Darryl and I returned to our separate lives on opposite coasts. The separation did not prevent us from communicating frequently, and a long-distance relationship ensued. When his work brought him anywhere close to the East Coast, he was sure to visit with me before returning to San Diego and vice-versa. Our work brought us together frequently at business meetings and conferences. I once traveled to St. Simons Island in Georgia for a week to relax and spend time with him while he was attending a meeting there.

Twice, Darryl arranged for me to fly to his home in San Diego to spend time together. It was during one of those romantic and unforgettable rendezvous that he brought up the subject of his hometown, platonic friend, Sharon Kraft. He explained that he told her about his relationship with me, and that she was planning a trip to Alexandria, Virginia, to visit her lover, Walter Pugh, a naval petty officer stationed at the Pentagon. Darryl asked if he could give Sharon my telephone number so that the two of us could meet when she was in my "neck of the woods." For a somewhat selfish reason, I was amenable to meeting her. Becoming acquainted with a close friend of his might give me more insight into this man, whom I held in high regard as a friend and professional colleague.

While a long-distance relationship with Darryl brought excitement and energy into my life, the distance was a barrier to anything sustainable. I thoroughly enjoyed our time together and the passion we shared. At times, he indicated that he would consider relocating to the East Coast — even going so far as looking into graduate schools in the DC area to close the distance between us. Because of my son, I was not interested in relocating to the West Coast. I had obligations in DC and he had ties in California that, as far as I was concerned, were too strong for either of us to break. If we had met at a different time and under different circumstances, who knows what could have happened. The reality was, however, that I did not want the pressure of a permanent relationship, and an ongoing serious relationship with Darryl was unrealistic.

Despite the obstacles in our relationship, I honored my promise to Darryl concerning his friend Sharon. The day she called me from her lover's apartment in Alexandria to introduce herself, we made plans to meet for lunch that weekend. We browsed boutiques and dined in a quaint restaurant in Adams Morgan, a culturally diverse community in Northwest DC. We spent hours getting acquainted and engaging in girl talk. There was something mysterious about this short, dark-brown-skinned woman with wide hips and an ample rear-end. It was annoyingly apparent that she suffered from nasal allergies, which caused her to blow her nose often and loudly. She talked incessantly about herself, appearing to be rather narcissistic. I must acknowledge that she had a lovely smile, with deep-set dimples in each cheek, and a neatly cropped Afro. To my surprise, she told me about her current marriage to Malcolm Kraft and her affair with Walter Pugh. Sharon stated emphatically, with no provocation from me, that she would not leave her husband for anyone. And there did not seem to be the least doubt in her mind that neither of her men would dare to leave her. This brazen woman seemed determined to leave no room for doubt that she had an iron grip on both her husband and her lover. She boasted about how she spent half of her time in San Diego with her husband and the other half in Alexandria with her lover — no questions asked or answered. Undoubtedly, I was confused as hell. Whatever the case, she was either one smooth cookie who qualified as an Academy Award-winning actress, or she was one cold, manipulative, and dangerous woman.

It was more than obvious that Sharon did whatever she wanted, and whenever she wanted. She was self-absorbed to the point that she believed she was entitled to lead a double, deceptive life. Surprisingly, I was indulging a woman who had similar characteristics of the abusive men that I had allowed into my life and married — egotistical, controlling, manipulative, and deceitful. I fulfilled my promise to Darryl to spend time with Sharon, but she was not the kind of person I would ever call a friend. I wondered what kind of man Walter Pugh was — this single man who played by a married woman's rules.

The answers to my questions began to unravel the evening I invited Sharon and Walter to my home for food and cocktails. She arrived with Petty Officer Walter Pugh, a medium-height, almost-white, easygoing, amicable man with a pleasing personality. After having made his acquaintance, I wondered why a kind and decent man would allow himself to be in an adulterous relationship with a narcissistic, controlling, disrespectful, married woman who, by her own admission, enjoyed jetting off to San Diego to be with her husband and leaving her lover with a stern admonishment that he heeded — "You'd better not be with anybody while I'm gone." Whatever needs Walter might have had in the interim were put on hold until she returned. Sharon was running two camps on two coasts. She was the one who decided when they would see each other again, and what Walter could and could not do while she was with her husband. My second sobering thought was, "Who was I to judge?" How dare I judge this man for being in an abusive relationship when I had been involved in numerous bad relationships.

Approximately one month after meeting Sharon and Walter, I was assigned to attend a meeting in San Diego. It was exactly what I needed — a chance for another romantic rendezvous with Darryl Barrow. When I arrived in San Diego, I was busy attending meetings during the day, and spending time with Darryl in the evenings. Before leaving home, I called Sharon to let her know that I would be in her town for a conference, and she immediately insisted that I be a guest in her home. I agreed to stay one night only and I must admit that Sharon and her husband, Malcolm, were wonderful hosts. I had observed her with Walter and now I had an opportunity to observe her with her husband. It was amazing to watch her play the role of the devoted wife right down to the last letter, while Malcolm Kraft, a tall, brown-skinned, handsome, quiet, and gracious man, appeared to be a husband who was content. Her ability to lead a double life with ease overwhelmed me. I tried to figure out how it was possible for her to manipulate her husband and her lover. Sharon, an abuser, chose her men like male abusers choose their victims. Malcolm was a carbon copy of Walter in temperament. Both were laid-back, cordial, and quiet. Both had Navy careers. As a matter of fact, she and

Walter had met in Puerto Rico two years prior and began their affair while Malcolm was deployed to sea duty.

I, of course, chose to spend the last night of my San Diego visit with Darryl. A few days after returning home, Darryl called to say he had accepted a job in Bakersfield, a city north of San Diego. He eventually married the woman with whom he was in a relationship, as expected.

Sharon and Walter began to have relationship problems. I recall an interesting conversation I had with Sharon during one of her visits to the East to spend time with Walter. She complained that Walter was very laid back and did not have the drive she needed in a man. I believe the reality is that they were both becoming weary of a relationship that was not fulfilling for either of them. I suspect that flying from coast to coast and scheming to hold onto two men more than likely became too costly and problematic to continue. I never learned the truth, but Walter and Sharon ended their relationship. He heard from her only once after their breakup. After that, she disappeared from his life — no questions asked, no questions answered.

Walter loved Sharon, and I knew he was in pain after their relationship ended because he would telephone me often to talk, and I could hear the hurt and disappointment in his voice. I listened to Walter and he listened to me. He heard my story and I heard his story. I made no judgment of Walter for putting up with Sharon's abuse, nor did he judge me for putting up with Derrick's abuse. In fact, Walter congratulated me for having the courage to leave him and start a new life.

During our long talks, I came to know and appreciate Walter's kindness. He was one of six children, three boys and three girls, and was born and raised in Lexington, Virginia, which he affectionately referred to as "Sexy Lex." His mother, fondly called "O," and his father, affectionately referred to as "Dirty," separated during Walter's childhood. It was interesting to learn that two of Walter's three sisters were victims of abuse by their husbands and partners. A proud career military man, Walter did not have a violent bone in his body — something new to me since practically every man in my life, including family, lovers, and friends, was either physically, emotionally, verbally, or mentally abusive. Like the men in my life, Walter enjoyed his libations and a good time; but unlike them, despite his life's disappointments, he chose to be positive. He lived by a "whatever" philosophy, refusing to let anything stress him to the point of losing control. To me, his calm essence was as soothing as a relaxing bath. Walter's military training and maturity brought a sense of order to his life and a semblance of order to mine.

Without saying it, Walter needed and wanted a friend, and so did I. He made it easy for me to lean on him and he lent an ear when I needed to talk. We both talked candidly about our lack of good judgment when it came to relationships. He thought of me as a caring person who made mistakes — no more and no less. He inspired me with gentle words of encouragement, things I needed to hear: "You're a smart woman." "You did not deserve to be treated the way your ex treated you." "You have so much potential and ambition." "You are somebody." I also gave him words of encouragement. We both knew we deserved better. We were able to acknowledge that we were wounded. There were times when Walter would stay overnight so that he would not be alone. He was offered the guest room, and I slept alone in my bedroom. When he stayed over, he would quietly leave in the morning, being careful not to disturb me. What we shared was comfort, reassurance, and respect, and a healthy, caring, supportive friendship blossomed.

In the subsequent days and months, it was only natural that our relationship would become deeper. Walter and I acknowledged that our feelings were growing beyond that of just friends, and the night came when Walter did not sleep in the guest bedroom. He slept with me in my bed and our intimacy did not damage our friendship. We were on the same wavelength. Neither one of us had marriage on our minds. Walter wanted at least two children and I chose to have a procedure to prevent pregnancy. Because of that, we both accepted that permanency was not in our future. Outside of his desire to eventually have children, Walter was happy with his nomadic military life, while I was beginning to learn how to be happy living my life as a single mom and as a woman free from the perpetual drama and chaos of abuse.

Yet, when Walter received orders to report to Oceana Naval Air Base in Virginia Beach, Virginia, I was sad, but relieved, that he would be only a short drive away and we could visit each other often. I honestly did not want to lose touch with my dear friend.

CHAPTER 18
HUSBAND NUMBER FOUR

L ack of funding ended my position at the nonprofit organization for runaway youth, and it was forced to close its doors. I was fortunate to be able to return to DC Public Schools as a bilingual education specialist, a position that came with immense pressure, but I enjoyed every minute of it. I was young and willing to take on challenges and responsibilities. I jumped in with both feet, learning the ropes, designing professional development courses for teachers, and working with the Hispanic community to partner with bilingual and English as a second language (ESL) school programs. I was professionally challenged and worked in a fast-paced, political environment. Financial security became my obsession. I wanted the best education for my son, to travel, and, more than anything, to not have to always worry about making ends meet. It was during this time that I learned that wealth does not come from a paycheck — it comes from entrepreneurship. I wanted to own a business where I called the shots, but that dream had to be put on hold for another time, as fate stepped in again.

Walter was now living and working in Virginia Beach, and we missed being together. During phone conversations, we frequently discussed ways to enhance our finances. I frequently stated that buying properties was a sure way to acquire wealth. We also talked about how marriage could help us financially. So, Walter and I decided to marry for economic reasons. We both understood that it was not a lifetime commitment.

In June 1984, we married at the Alexandria, Virginia, courthouse, marking the beginning of our "partnership." My new husband was still stationed in Virginia Beach, but came home every weekend and on holidays. Shortly after we married, interest rates were usurious due to "Reaganomics," but Walter and I made our first investment — a cute one-bedroom condo in Southwest DC. While I was putting my innate interior designer's touch on the condo and transforming it into an oasis, I was planning our next real estate purchase. We had a marriage made from friendship and a desire to acquire wealth together. For that reason, we were content. My husband was kind, gentle, and considerate.

Being a sailor's wife was a completely different world for me. It was a totally different life and there was much to learn about military etiquette. Aside from those days of sheer pandemonium when the spouses of sailors flocked to the docks to say goodbye at deployments and welcome their loved ones returning home from sea, military life was about order, regimen, and rules. To this day, I applaud military families who can keep it all together.

It takes a special breed of people to live the military life. I detest regimen — it's boring and gets in the way of my free nature. Authority is necessary, but I prefer to call my own shots. I can recall my first trip to the commissary, which alone was a major culture shock. I was accustomed to showing identification when shopping and using my credit card or when pulled over for a traffic violation. It took a while to become accustomed to showing military ID for everything, e.g., shopping, medical, NCO clubs, credit union, etc. I understood the reason for showing my ID, but it got on my last nerve. Unlike civilian grocery stores where I could maneuver my shopping cart up and down any aisle of my choice, military commissaries require shoppers to follow arrows designating the direction in which to push the cart.

Another undeniable and particularly unnerving aspect of military life was the high rate of adultery and domestic violence. Grateful that my days of abuse were behind me, I thanked God that my life with Walter was completely absent of violence. We did not so much as engage in arguments. Of course, we had our share of disagreements — he would stress his opinions and I would voice mine, but he never raised his voice at me or called me out of my name.

I thought things were going just too well in my life, and began to worry that something was about to happen. Just prior to my marriage, a long-time nagging pain in my lower right abdomen seemed to be diminishing. I had seen a number of physicians about the pain; they told me it was probably a cyst and there was nothing to worry about. Walter told me that as a military spouse, I would get the best medical care whenever I needed it. He joked that spouses received better care than enlisted members. I decided to see an Army gynecologist for an examination. Walter made the appointment for me with a gynecologist at Walter Reed Army Medical Center. Dr. Rose Liu was a petite Asian woman. She was a lovely person, warm and friendly, with a contagious sense of humor and an enviable bedside manner. After she examined me and did a Pap smear, she asked me to wait in her office. A short while later, she entered the room wearing a smile and carrying the chart on which she made notes as we engaged in a question-and-answer session about my general health.

Everything was going along fine until I told her about the pain, though now barely noticeable, in my lower right abdomen. She stopped taking notes, appeared to be in deep thought, and then said, "Let's get you back on the table." I undressed and got back on the examination table, while Dr. Liu guided my feet into the stirrups. She sat down on the examination stool, and placed a Pap stick deep into my uterus. Nothing was typical or routine about the second Pap smear. I was totally unprepared for the excruciating pain that felt like it shot through every nerve in my body. I let out a deep moan. Dr. Liu helped me down from the table, instructed me to get dressed again, and informed that she would call me with the test results. I didn't give it a second thought — none of the other tests showed anything abnormal. I was feeling better than I had been in many months. I went about enjoying my new abuse-free married life until the phone call from Dr. Liu changed everything.

I was in a meeting when I was informed that I had an important phone call. It was Dr. Liu.

"Mrs. Pugh?" Dr. Liu asked.

"Yes," I hesitantly responded.

"I have the results of your Pap smear. I have good news and bad news," she guardedly said. "The bad news is that your test reveals that you have severe dysphasia in your cervix."

"What does that mean?" I asked.

Dr. Liu explained that severe dysphasia was a last stage before cancer. She then went on to tell me the good news. "The good news is that I believe we caught it in time." Needless to say, the good news was drowned out by the bad, and I lost all composure in the hallway of the Gordon School. I telephoned Walter at the naval base, and, trying to hold back my tears, shared what Dr. Liu had just disclosed. He immediately left Virginia Beach and headed home.

The mystery, according to Dr. Liu, was that the result of the Pap smear indicated that there were three dysphasic spots in my cervix, one of which was severely dysphasic — a prelude to cervical cancer. More tests were ordered, but the renegade severe dysphasia spot could not be located.

Walter and I made the decision that I would resign from my position with DCPS, rent the condo, and move to Virginia Beach to be with him so that he could take care of me. We hired a real estate agent and began the search for a house in Virginia Beach. We found a comfortable duplex townhouse that was 15 minutes from the beach. I love the beach and having it so accessible was like having a piece of heaven on Earth in the midst of a storm.

Dr. Liu made arrangements to have my medical file transferred to Portsmouth Naval Hospital in Portsmouth, Virginia — thirty-five minutes from Virginia Beach — and made arrangements for me to immediately see a specialist there. I was not in denial about the seriousness of my condition. I always stood toe-to-toe with adversity and I would not fold now. My only fear was that I would not see my baby boy grow up. I prayed fervently for God to allow me to live to see my son become a man.

At Portsmouth Naval Hospital, my case was assigned to Dr. Penelope McDonald, a white lieutenant surgeon. After three months of more tests, the dysphasic spot was finally located high up in the cervix. I was admitted into the hospital two days later for surgery. After the surgery, through a fog, I heard my surgeon telling Walter that there were no complications. Then I heard her tell me that the surgery went well as she coaxed me to open my eyes. I wanted her to go away, to let me sleep; it was totally impossible to open my eyes. Didn't she understand that? Finally, I found the energy to barely crack open one eye — it was like moving a mountain. I immediately went back to sleep. Periodically, the nurses would wake me.

The next morning, still groggy from the anesthesia, I opened my eyes to see Walter sitting next to my bed. I felt someone rubbing my head, and made out the figure of a woman as I struggled to open my eyes. The woman leaned over closer and kissed me on the forehead. "Everything turned out fine. You are going to be okay." I turned to the sound of my husband's voice. He looked very tired, but relieved. He never left the hospital, staying there all night with me. He was sitting there and smiling as I was trying to wake up. "The doctor removed your uterus and right ovary. You're going to be all right," he said again. In that moment, I prayed. I thanked God for giving me a second chance to see my son grow into manhood.

The next day when Walter came to check on me, I asked him if it was my mother I saw after the surgery or was it a dream. He laughed and said, "Yeah, Betty is here. She's going to stay with us for a week to take care of you. Don't worry about anything," he said. "Just rest." God, when did anybody tell me to just rest? When I was released from the hospital, my mother was waiting at our house. She had cooked and tidied up the place. Unfortunately, I was still too sick and my body too fragile to digest a heavy meal. But Walter made sure my mother's cooking did not go to waste.

Shortly after I was released from the hospital, my father called to say he was coming to see me. Sick of being trapped in the bedroom and eager to see my father, I asked Walter to prepare a place on the couch in the living room and help me downstairs where I hoped to spend the day.

When Daddy arrived, I could tell by the look on his face that he was shocked to see how sick I was. He tried to hide his expression, but I knew I looked like death walking. I had lost a lot of weight, was pale as a ghost, and could barely move without help. I was a pitiful sight. He managed to stay with me from eleven o'clock Sunday morning until seven-thirty that night — a major feat for a man who could not tolerate sickness. But in that short visit, for the first time, I saw past the harsh, no-nonsense, take-no-prisoners attitude of a ruthless hustler to the heart of a father who loved his daughter. Perhaps a year or more later, Daddy confided that he thought I was on my deathbed — "I couldn't stand it," he said.

As for my mother, I like to think that maybe for the first time she recognized that "Miss Independent" did need her. She buzzed around the house like a busy bee — cooking, cleaning, and administering my prescribed medication on schedule, and catching up on her favorite soap operas. Still, I sensed my mother was uncomfortable when it was only the two of us, because during her weeklong stay, we shared little more than polite conversation. Most of the time, I was confined to the upstairs bedroom. When Walter came home from work, the two of them ate, looked at television, and talked.

Although I know my mother was concerned about my health, she was also worried sick about her precious son, who was incarcerated again. She made it perfectly clear that she had to get back to DC, and I knew not to even suggest that she consider extending her visit. No matter how much my brother disrespected our mother, even when she visited him in jail, nothing was going to get in the way of her being available for her treasured, demonic, jailbird son. She needed to be near him because she knew he needed her to take care of him.

While Walter drove my mother to the airport to catch her flight back to DC, Aunt Eunice and her daughter, Pamela, arrived to help out for the weekend. I was ecstatic to see them and enjoyed their company. Aunt Eunice was the liveliest of my mother's rambunctious sisters, and her daughter, Pamela, who is nine years older than I am, seemed to be happy to be there to help me, talking about old times and coming up with ways to make me laugh and smile. Pamela, another fantastic cook, prepared a delectable dish of liver, onions, gravy, and rice — a family favorite. I savored every morsel and Walter was in heaven. It was wonderful to have family around who truly wanted to be there. I relished every second with Aunt Eunice and Pamela, but their weekend visit came to an end

Husband Number Four

way too soon. I cried when they left, feeling sick and alone because Walter had to work.

I continued to recover from the surgery in the quiet of my bedroom, occasionally watching television. On the morning of January 28, 1986, I was captivated by the televised liftoff of the Space Shuttle Challenger. There was an inescapable excitement about this voyage. Aboard this shuttle was Christie McAuliffe, the first member of the NASA Teacher in Space Program. I watched and listened to every historic moment — the countdown, the anxious crowd of spectators, the thunderous roar of the engine launching the spacecraft off the ground at Cape Canaveral into the blue skies above the Atlantic Ocean — then the earth-shattering, thunderous boom. Next, I heard gasps of horror and disbelief in the voices of news reporters acknowledging, analyzing, and then confirming the confusing messages broadcasted from NASA Control engineers. My eyes remained frozen to the set for what seemed like an eternity. I, too, was in a state of shock. I didn't want to believe what I saw. The Space Shuttle Challenger, within seconds of takeoff, exploded and disintegrated. I lay in bed praying that the shuttle had not exploded — it had to be a problem with the broadcast. But it was true, and all seven of the astronaut crew, five men and two women, were dead.

Death is a part of life that is at first easier to deny than to face, but having recently had my own brush with death, I was extremely sensitive to this tragedy. I prayed for the astronauts; prayed they never felt one twinge of pain; prayed for their families. I was filled with gratitude that I was given a second chance at life. And while it can be argued that the surgery prevented me from developing full-blown ovarian and cervical cancer, I know it was God who pulled me through. No longer facing the nightmare of battling a vicious illness that threatened to end my life at thirty-five, I was extremely grateful that God had seen fit to grant me a second chance and the opportunity to strengthen my relationship with Him and the people who were important in my life.

Richard, my precious son who was now ten, was a serious-minded child living with his dad and growing up fast. Without knowing it, he taught me the joy and pain of motherhood. In my moments of meditation, I thanked God for the time He allowed me to share with my son, hearing my son's voice and him hearing mine. Every event in Richard's life, whether it was a good report card or one that required encouragement for more study; or his tears resulting from a fall, a cut on his knee; his laughter, the pride in his face after a successful karate class, all are engraved in my heart. How grateful I was for every time I heard him tell me "I love you" or for every time I told him that I loved him is beyond words. To this day, I vividly remember my prayer to God asking Him to allow me to see my son grow from childhood to manhood. He answered my prayer and I am more than thankful.

My husband and dear friend did not once complain about the enormous financial responsibility placed on him during my lengthy illness because I was unable to work. The day Walter and I decided to marry, there was no doubt in my mind that he was sincere about doing what was best for the both of us. Never in a hundred years did I imagine that he would have to sacrifice so much at the start of our life together. He accepted the curveball life had thrown our way, but I was not blind to the effect of my illness on him. There were times when I saw the financial pressure he was under as a result of my inability to work. Yet, he continually assured me that everything was under control and that I should not worry about anything except getting well. Never wavering in his commitment, he hung in there with me through my illness every step of the way — like the man and soldier he was. To this day, when my mind wanders back, I recall when we stood before the justice of the peace and pledged our vows. There is no question that we both got far more than we bargained for, but the worst was not over — there was another rocky mountain yet to climb.

CHAPTER 19

ANOTHER MEDICAL SETBACK

Three weeks after my surgery, I was scheduled to see Dr. Penelope McDonald for a post-operative exam. I was feeling better and I thought I was having a relatively good recovery. Walter and I were escorted to her office and asked to have a seat. When she entered, I sensed something was wrong. Cordial greetings were exchanged as she slowly pulled the high-back chair back away from the desk and gently lowered herself into it. Opening a file on her desk, Dr. McDonald asked how I was feeling and told me I looked like I was doing well. She explained the surgical procedure to us as a lead-in to what she knew I did not want to hear. During the surgery, she explained, my left ovary appeared to be perfectly healthy, and she made the decision to leave it because she did not want me to go into premature menopause. However, she went on to tell us, to be on the safe side, she ordered a biopsy of the left ovary. Unfortunately, she continued, the biopsy indicated that the same dysphasic cells that existed in my right ovary and cervix were also in my left ovary. In essence, a second surgery was needed. I sat frozen — unable to fathom what she was telling me. The doctor recommended that I wait 30 days before undergoing a second major invasive operation.

When we left the office, I was still in a state of shock. At home, I broke down and cried, "Another surgery! I can't go through another surgery! I just can't! I'm not strong enough! This time I will die! I just know it!" All my husband could do was hold me and try to comfort me as best he could until I could pull myself together. After deciding what I wanted to do about my health, I calmly told Walter that I wanted to return home to DC. I wanted to have the second surgery at Walter Reed Army Medical Center, where I would be closer to family and friends — my support group. "If that's what you want to do," he replied, "then that's what we'll do." Luckily, our tenant's lease was up and we just needed to provide a thirty-day notice to vacate the premises. I can vividly recall thinking what a wonderful man I had married. Without a hint of anger, frustration, or reluctance, arrangements were made for my move back to our condo in DC and for the surgery to take place at Walter Reed.

Our tenant had not maintained the DC property and it needed extensive repair, which Walter coordinated in several trips to DC. A few days before my scheduled surgery, I was back home, but the day I left our Virginia Beach home, I felt a strange sense of sadness.

The day before the surgery, I checked into Walter Reed and met my new surgeon, Dr. Lisa Sinclair, for the first time. She was a young, dainty blond with a warm personality. I was impressed with her knowledge of my medical history. It was almost as if she had been on the journey with me the entire time. I liked her immediately and I was at ease with her as my surgeon. By now, I preferred female gynecologists because of their compassion. After all, it was a female, Dr. Rose Liu, who, after a brief consultation, understood the necessity to check further based on what I disclosed about my symptoms.

At Walter Reed, a team of doctors reviewed my medical history. Two male doctors, who would be instrumental in assisting Dr. Sinclair, met with me the night before the surgery. The anesthesiologist explained to me in precise detail the procedure of "putting me under" and what I could expect when I woke up. That conversation was the easy one. The second doctor, an oncologist, discussed options for treatment after surgery, should my condition warrant radiation or chemotherapy. What I knew for a fact about chemotherapy is that everyone in my family who underwent it died shortly thereafter from complications from the toxic drugs. I listened politely, carefully and attentively, but my mind was already made up. When he finished, I politely told the oncologist "no, thank you" to chemotherapy. I flatly refused to hear any more about it and adamantly told him it was needless to bring it up again. Chemotherapy would not be an option for me. Doctors do not know everything, but there was one thing I knew for sure: My family cannot tolerate chemotherapy. Actually, not many people can. I let it be known that if it was found that I had cancer, I would choose quality of life rather than to be unimaginably sick and burdensome as a result of chemotherapy, and die anyway.

On the morning of my surgery, Dr. Sinclair came to my room to see me before the operation. I was a bundle of nerves, crumbling into a thousand emotional pieces, and crying incessantly. The harder I tried to stop sobbing, the harder I cried. I cannot explain how I felt except to say that it was a fear of the unknown. Dr. Sinclair clasped my hand in hers, and reassured me in a calm, soothing voice that I was going to be just fine. Again, I cried harder. I was petrified. The 30-day waiting period had supposedly given my body time to regain enough strength, but it did nothing to ease my fragile state of mind. I barely made it through the first surgery. How could I do it again? The mere thought of opening the same incision and taking out more of my reproductive organs was asking a bit too much. I just did not see how I could survive a second major operation. I couldn't grasp it.

My first surgeon in Portsmouth had obviously not been interested in making the incision cosmetically appealing. Since I had to have a second surgery, reopening the same incision, why not get a freebie, I thought to myself. Being vain, I said to my young surgeon, "Since you have to re-open the prior incision, it would be much appreciated if you would make my incision more cosmetically appealing." She looked at me and smiled, "I'll see what I can do."

I was fearful that I would not make it through the second surgery. I thought death was all around me. I felt death. I now know it was depression. As I was wheeled down the hall and into the elevator that was to take me down to the surgical suite, I looked over at Dr. Sinclair, who I trusted would do her best to bring me through the surgery. I prayed to see my son and Walter again. Once inside the surgical suite, I was prepped for the procedure. Still, I could not stop crying, but Dr. Sinclair calmly reassured me that everything would be fine. When she realized that I could not stop crying, she gave a subtle nod to the anesthesiologist. After that nod, the lights were out.

Soon, I was awakened by my doctor gently coaxing me to open my eyes. When I heard her say that the surgery was successful, I struggled with all my might to open my eyes. After a few efforts and her coaxing, I managed to barely crack open my eyes, very briefly. Dr. Sinclair sensed that I was trying to tell her something. She lowered her ear to my mouth. Forcing out words, I whispered, "My back hurts." Pain medication was immediately administered. Within seconds, I drifted off into a peaceful sleep — one that caused me often to wonder if that is indeed what death is like. If so, then I submit unequivocally that there is no reason for anyone to be afraid to die when the time comes. I just wasn't ready, not right then. Besides God sparing my life for the second time, Dr. Sinclair did an excellent cosmetic repair to the previous abdominal incision. It was barely visible. She told me that it was her gift to me, and I often think of the young woman who helped me through a second painful surgery. She left a great impression on me. Women are awesome!

To me, recovering from the second surgery was by far worse than the first. The day after the surgery, a nurse came to my room and told me I had to be moved to a chair. I was exhausted, weak, and sick. I didn't want to be bothered — just let me sleep, that's all I wanted. I most surely could not get out of the bed, but over my objections and tears, I was helped out of bed and into a nearby chair. Trying to get to the chair was equivalent to walking one hundred miles barefoot after being shot. "Come on, you're doing just great! Only a few more steps," was her chant. All I could think about was what I wanted to do to her!

Four days after surgery, I was released from the hospital. I continue to be amazed at how patients are sent home from the hospital half-dead from surgery. I was sick as hell when I was released. According to Walter, the second surgery seemed easier on me than the first. But what I endured after the first surgery paled in comparison to the hell I lived through after the second surgery. On the afternoon Walter brought me home from the hospital, I developed severe gas pains in my stomach. The pains were so intense I thought I might need to be rushed back to the hospital. I needed relief — I couldn't handle the pain. Walter rushed across the street to the neighborhood drugstore to talk with the pharmacist on duty.

The pharmacist suggested an over-the-counter medicine for severe gas discomfort, which, thankfully, worked.

No matter how difficult the challenges, the old saying that there is something good in everything definitely applied to my life. It was a turning point for me. Again, God granted my request to live to see my son grow to be a man and I was intent on showing Him my gratitude for the precious gift of life. I made up my mind that I would be a faithful servant, change my unhealthy diet, treat my body as a temple, practice patience and humility, and live a stress-free life. I would learn to relinquish my troubles to Him.

I was ready and willing to experience all that life had to offer me with the intention of sharing my newfound zest for life with Walter and Richard. But when you think everything is finally on the up-and-up, something comes along to knock it down — life is like that!

CHAPTER 20
HUSBAND NUMBER FIVE
YES, WE DID IT TWICE

Walter received new orders during my recuperation from the second surgery. This time he was deployed to New Orleans, which was fine with me because New Orleans was a short flight compared to international flights, but I knew I would miss him. Temporary separation is a reality for military families and I had to deal with that. As a part of regaining my strength, Walter and I would walk around the neighborhood and sometimes take a longer walk to the wharf. We often talked about our future — I envisioned living abroad with him before he retired from the Navy. Before Walter left for New Orleans, he rented our home in Virginia Beach. I maintained the Southwest condo, and he took care of our rental property in Virginia Beach. I received an allotment check each month that made my life relatively comfortable. I was happy about that; it was a new experience to get an allowance from my husband. Walter also periodically deposited funds into my account at the Navy Federal Credit Union for any additional needs. For the first time, I began to experience what security felt like. Free medical care, allotment checks, commissary privileges, travel abroad, and two properties. For months, my husband and I spoke often by phone and one of us would grab a flight to spend time together.

On one occasion, Walter was deployed to Spain. After being there for an extended period of time, he requested and was granted a weeklong furlough. He asked me to fly to Spain to join him, and I was excited to see him. I felt like a newlywed. It would be my first international flight alone. He made arrangements for us to meet and vacation for one week on a beautiful Spanish island, Palma de Mallorca — a great place to relax, dine, and enjoy the beach. It was a tourist site, away from crowds and the noise of Madrid. We stayed in a small, lovely, quaint hotel overlooking a beautiful unspoiled beach. Europeans, I learned, are wonderfully uninhibited folks. People walked along the beach nude from the waist up. Nude children were running, playing, and screaming with glee. This magical Spanish island was one that offered freedom of expression, an environment that suited me perfectly. There was never a dull moment for us. We browsed the shops and purchased leather outfits, pearls, jewelry, and mementos for our home. We looked forward to the afternoon siestas and would find a quiet restaurant and lunch on cool gazpacho, seafood, and *vino tinto* (red wine). We were careful not to eat too much during the day because the heavy meals were reserved for late evenings, as is the culture in Spain. Time flew, and before we knew it, it was time for Walter to return to his ship and for me to return to the United States. However, we found satisfaction in knowing that he would be home soon — at least back in the states.

Shortly after Walter returned to New Orleans, everything changed. I didn't know what happened, but I did not want to lose my husband or my military benefits. He began to find reasons not to come home to visit and made excuses why it was not a good time for me to visit him in New Orleans. It was driving me insane. The very few times he came home, we did not have sex. He was his normal self until it was time for intimacy. I continuously asked him what was wrong, but he would not give me an answer — only that "it's me and not you." I thought perhaps he might be gay or had contracted some disease that he didn't want to tell me about. It wasn't long before he stopped coming home altogether. I ceased trying to find out what was wrong. Eventually, he went on to live his life in New Orleans and I lived a single life in DC. It didn't take a rocket scientist to realize that my marriage was over, but I didn't know why. It clearly did not make sense for me to remain in a marriage with a man who made it quite clear that he was ready to move on. After all, I had fully recuperated.

I believed Walter was waiting for me to end our marriage, so I called him at work and told him I was filing for a divorce. He did not object.

Because the agreement to separate was amicable, I personally prepared and filed the divorce papers. Our divorce was final in March 1988. We agreed that I would keep the condo and he would keep the property in Virginia Beach. Neither one of us was bitter or angry. It was a business arrangement anyway. I knew I had a lot to thank him for — the four years of friendship, support, medical care, properties, and security. It was more than I ever had.

A few months after our divorce, Walter drove from New Orleans to Alexandria, Virginia, to visit his sister. At the time, I was working as a freelance legal secretary for a law firm in Washington, DC. I planned to open a temporary placement company for legal secretaries and decided to get as much inside information and experience about law firms as possible. He called me while in Virginia and wanted to take me to lunch. I was happy to hear from my ex-husband and agreed to have lunch with him. He picked me up at 12:30 p.m., and I noticed after a while that we were in Alexandria, which I assumed was because he was familiar with the area. But, when I saw that he was going to the courthouse, I asked, "What the hell are we doing here?"

He replied, "Getting married again."

"What? Are you crazy? We just got divorced," I replied.

In his logical manner, Walter said, "It's for financial reasons. I get more money if I'm married, and it will help you because you will be eligible for spousal military benefits again." It was true that I was having my share of financial woes without the additional income I had come to depend on, so his "no strings attached" business arrangement offer was one that I could live with. I certainly was not thinking of marrying again. By 2:00 p.m., I was married to Walter Pugh for a second time, but it was strictly a business arrangement that did not include visits or sex. Marrying for love and a happy family did not seem to do anything for me but cause distress, so why not go for the security?

Walter was still living and working in New Orleans. He loved "sin city" — the parties, booze, women, and food. I moved forward with my life as a "single" woman with a guaranteed monthly allotment from an invisible husband. But we continued to stay in touch by phone and occasional cards.

We had been married for six years the second time when one day, as I was going through the mail, I saw an official-looking envelope. It was a Petition for Absolute Divorce. It knocked the wind out of me. Walter was divorcing me. I could not believe it. I was stunned and pissed off. Why he chose to inform me in that manner was a mystery to me. I was beyond angry with Walter for not being forthright and letting me know what his plans were before sending divorce papers, so I immediately telephoned him to let him know how I felt. He apologized, saying that he did not know how to tell me he was ready for a divorce. I asked him if he wanted a divorce to marry someone else. "No!" he replied. I agreed to the divorce and wished him well. I thanked him for the years of allotment checks and free medical care.

Husband Number Five

CHAPTER 21
ENTREPRENEURSHIP

In June 1988, Chappelle Services, Inc. (CSI), a company specializing in the placement of legal secretaries on a temporary and permanent basis in prestigious law firms in the Washington, DC, metropolitan area, officially opened for business. With my health back on track, having bachelor's and master's degrees and no permanent job, I decided to venture into the world of entrepreneurship. It made perfect sense to me to market my business skills, given my desire to make use of my under graduate minor in business education. The timing couldn't have been better to pursue my unspoken dream of owning a business. During that time, there was a critical shortage of experienced legal secretaries in the Washington metropolitan area.

In a way, I went back to my roots. I began my business slowly — initially as a freelance or contract legal secretary. From the start, I was blown away by the exorbitant hourly rate I could charge law firms and how willingly they paid for my services without any hassle. My first contract was with a medium-sized law firm in downtown DC. It was not long before information about my service began to spread, and I quickly began to get freelance offers from various prestigious law firms of all sizes. The workload soon grew beyond what I could handle alone. I began to recruit people with basic legal secretarial experience, trained them, and dispatched them on job assignments that I was too busy to accept. Law firms that hired CSI temporary employees to work for their firms on a permanent basis paid CSI a large placement fee.

In 1989, I hung out my shingle in the heart of downtown DC on the "Eye" Street corridor, near a host of bustling law firms. My initial office space, located in an old apartment building that had been renovated into an office building, was formerly a huge one-bedroom apartment. Because of my ties to the legal community, I received a pro bono review of the office lease, and signed it with confidence. Wood floors were stained, the bathroom lavishly decorated, and I arranged to have the rooms painted in warm, welcoming colors. I love color and spent days on end selecting the right office furniture, telephone services, stationery, business cards, and countless other minute details to successfully set up and operate an efficient and organized business. It seemed that everything was falling into place.

I hired Malcolm Bradley as my office manager and collector of past-due accounts. Malcolm turned out to be an exceptional and loyal employee who possessed in-depth technical knowledge. But within six months of occupying my first office space, the effects of "Reaganomics" began to slow the nation's economy, making it difficult for CSI to obtain contracts. The recession forced small businesses, particularly service-oriented minority businesses, to close their doors. The once-bustling office building that housed CSI now closely resembled a ghost town, its halls dark and quiet. My company was beginning to gross much less, and I struggled to meet payroll and keep the doors open.

However, there was an upside to the economic downturn. Because businesses were quickly folding, office space was being leased at reduced, bargain-basement prices per square foot, so I did not renew my lease on the "Eye" Street corridor — which had become known as the "hospital for sick businesses" — and moved into an office space with more modern, up-to-date amenities, on Vermont Avenue. Though my second office was not as spacious as the first, there was an inescapable charm about it. I felt an air of success the day I first stepped into the new, more upscale downtown lobby and saw my company's name on the marquee. It felt like I had finally "made it."

Malcolm Bradley and I got to work like busy bees setting up the new office and notifying CSI clients of our change of address. But despite our tireless efforts, the recession began to hit us harder. No money was coming in and CSI was sinking faster than a leaking boat under the crunch of a failing economy. Then a miracle happened — CSI was thrown a life preserver.

A downtown law firm was changing its computer software system and needed legal secretaries while its staff was being trained on new software. The firm provided CSI with a lucrative 90-day contract. While this was a desperately needed shot of adrenaline, it was too little and too late to fully resuscitate the company. CSI was making money again, but not enough to catch up on delinquent employee taxes, other business-related debt, expenses, and overhead — not to mention that I had not paid myself in months.

On another day, I received a call from a high-profile law firm in need of long-term legal secretarial support. I immediately gave the assignment to Heather Wilkinson, a new CSI employee who had top notch legal secretarial skills. I was more than relieved. Unfortunately, relief quickly turned to utter disbelief and professional humiliation. Heather was as beautiful as she was smart and skilled, but she was an alcoholic who had managed from the day she was hired to hide her illness until she showed up for work intoxicated and reeking of liquor. Nevertheless, the firm was so impressed with her skills that the administrator offered to pay for Heather to join a rehabilitation program. I jumped at the deal, but in my heart I knew it would not work out.

The deal was not etched in stone, because the contract provided for thirty days of probation before CSI would be paid the placement fee. All I could do was cross my fingers, hope, and pray for the best. She did not make it to thirty days. Heather messed up again by not showing up for work. The law firm's administrator called to advise me she was not satisfied with the placement and requested a full refund of the placement fee. I was at my wit's end, and called Heather at home. Her mother answered and said, "She's asleep." I hesitantly, but briefly, explained that Heather was employed by an important CSI client and that she had not shown up for work that morning. "Didn't Heather tell you she was an alcoholic?" her mother asked in a puzzled voice. "Her father was an alcoholic."

Before I could recover from the fiasco involving Heather Wilkinson, I was faced with another employee-related setback. Carlton Beamon was a handsome young man, immaculately dressed, and a proficient legal secretary. I placed him in a temporary assignment at another well-known, highly respected firm. Shortly after beginning his assignment, the firm decided to hire him. Just days after the decision to hire Carlton, he became ill and had to be hospitalized. The law firm's administrator telephoned me to inquire about his medical status. I called his home and spoke to Carlton's father. "Carlton won't be returning to work," his father said. "My son has full-blown AIDS." Poor Carlton.

By 1992, CSI was dying a slow death. Bills were past due, IRS was hounding me for back taxes, and I had no money for personal living expenses. I had exhausted what little savings I had left to keep the company afloat. Earlier that year, I borrowed $20,000 from a venture capitalist using the condo that I owned as collateral. It was not a smart thing to do because I needed much more than $20,000 to stay above water as a result of the recession. It was not long before I was penniless and forced to apply for Chapter 7 bankruptcy protection. I surrendered my lovely condo and had no alternative but to rent an apartment in a friend's name. The bankruptcy allowed me to keep my 1986 Saab, but because I was broke, I could not make the car payments. My financial troubles were far from resolved so my only alternative was to hide the car wherever I could, within long walking distance of my apartment, for nearly a year to avoid the "snatch man."

The recession made it almost impossible to find employment. In a quest to survive, I returned to work as a contract legal secretary wherever I could. Many law firms either merged to survive or closed their doors. Thankfully, though, a few law firms managed to maintain their business, but not to the extent of the past. My contracts were sporadic and short, some one week out of a month. The firms especially liked having me aboard because, as a contractor, they did not have to provide benefits for me and I knew the business like the back of my hand.

After losing the condo, I moved into a two-bedroom duplex apartment on Capitol Hill in Northeast DC. My financial troubles were more than a nightmare. My son was now in college. Whatever hardship I was facing, I remained committed to fulfilling my financial obligation to keep him in school.

During my time at the "hospital for sick businesses," I became acquainted with a woman who worked in the same building. During one of our conversations, she told me that she wanted to move out of her parents' home. I needed someone with whom to share the rent. It was not long before we became roommates. Henrietta Murphy was a hefty, divorced African American woman with a beautifully round, brown face and an electric smile. Gorgeous prematurely gray hair framed her face.

In addition to her nine-to-five office job, Henrietta was a gifted singer who performed with her father and sisters at church programs, weddings, and funerals. I know I made bad decisions when it came to men, but Henrietta did not have a shred of common sense in that department. She dated men who disrespected and blatantly mistreated her from the beginning. For example, she began to spend time with Carl, her ex-husband, who was addicted to drugs. Whenever he came around, he stayed in her bedroom behind closed doors — never venturing out except to go to the bathroom or leave the apartment. Chills would creep up my spine when he was around. It was something about him that I did not trust, but I refrained from commenting on her personal life.

One evening, she asked, and I agreed, to let her borrow my fur coat to wear to a play that she was attending with her drug-addicted ex-husband. Shortly after they left for the play, I went out to run a few errands. When I returned to the apartment, I knew immediately that the apartment had been burglarized because my stereo system was gone and a few other items were nowhere to be found. The burglars entered the ground-floor apartment through an unlocked window — a window that I never unlocked. There was no doubt in my mind that Henrietta's ex-husband was responsible for the burglary. When they returned to the apartment, I told them what had happened. Henrietta was visibly shaken. When we were alone, I verbalized my suspicion about Carl's involvement with the theft, which, of course, put a strain on our relationship. I did not spend much time talking about the theft because I was still knee-deep in debt and could not afford the rent by myself.

One morning shortly after the burglary incident, I came downstairs and saw Henrietta packing boxes. Surprised, I asked, "What are you doing?"

"I'm moving," she replied, nonchalantly.

"Without giving me any notice?" I angrily asked.

"Yes," she said, and then went on to advise me that she and her drug-addicted ex-husband were moving together again. "He found us an apartment," she said.

"So, what am I supposed to do about your share of the rent?" I asked.

She shrugged her shoulders, and continued packing boxes while waiting for Carl to show up with the moving truck, but he never came for her. Henrietta paced for hours, peeping out the window and anxiously waiting for him to arrive. Her embarrassment and stupidity were a sight to behold. Eventually she loaded the boxes in her car, and since she had no way to move her bedroom set, she left, saying, "I'll come back for the bedroom set later." After a few days, she called to let me know that she was coming to get her bedroom set. I reminded her that she did not fulfill her agreement to me regarding thirty days' notice before moving. I informed her that until she paid her share of the rent, I would not surrender her bedroom set.

Weeks passed before she telephoned me to tell me that she had the money that was owed to me, and asked if she could pick up the bedroom set. We agreed on a time and date for her to retrieve the furniture. When she arrived, it was obvious that she was uncomfortable. We spoke cordially and I invited her and a male companion into the apartment to move her bedroom furniture. While there, she confessed that she never saw nor heard from Carl since the last time he was at our apartment. She also shared with me that she had wanted to come back, but was too embarrassed to ask me. I told her that could never have happened anyway. "All I want is for you to get your bedroom set and get the hell out of my apartment," I said.

CHAPTER 22
TAKING CARE OF DADDY

As early as 1988, the same year CSI opened for business, I noticed that my father's usual fast, spirited pace was changing — he was moving slower. We met routinely for lunch at Scholl's Restaurant on 19th Street NW, a short walk from a law firm at 20th and K Streets, where I had a long-term contract. During one of our father-daughter lunches, Daddy told me that he had been seeing a urologist for the past three years and had undergone several minor procedures. He said confidently, "There's nothing to worry about." I believed him because it was easier, so we filled our conversations with business plans and other general conversation. Of course, when the conversation focused on me, I would tell him how well the freelance business was doing. My world always seemed a lot better seeing his smile of approval. Although I was grown, my father's opinion of me was extremely important.

In 1989, after a series of hospital stays, Daddy was diagnosed with bladder cancer. He hesitantly underwent surgery to remove the cancerous bladder. The day following his surgery, he awoke to his new reality. The doctors replaced his bladder with a urine bag that was attached to his right side. I believe he was in a serious state of shock after the surgery when faced with the reality that he had to learn to live with a "bag" until he died. The reality hit him like a ton of bricks. He telephoned me one evening after he had been released from the hospital, crying uncontrollably. "Baby, they done cut me all to pieces."

With tears in my eyes, I encouraged my father to be strong, to hang on; expressed my happiness that he was still alive; and assured him that

I would always be there for him. It was a commitment that I meant and a commitment that I kept. During his recuperation period, I went to his apartment every day to help him and to give Miss Maye, the woman Daddy considered "ugly and not his type," a break from the nonstop care she provided even though she was ill with colon cancer. The previous year, Miss Maye had undergone colon surgery. For six months, she was forced to wear a colostomy bag until her colon healed enough for it to be removed.

The most frustrating part of taking care of Daddy was changing his urine bag. The bag had to be attached with special tape to a piece of flesh in his side. Human flesh is extremely soft, wet, and slippery. It was a frustrating chore fumbling to hold onto the flesh and tape the urine bag securely to it. When I would finally get the bag on, I would go into the bathroom and sob. As proud as my father was, he was now relegated to peeing in a bag. After his surgery, the doctors gave Daddy three years to live.

Daddy enjoyed his life during his youth when he had money and his share of fine clothes, young women, and fancy cars. Now he was old, sick, and broke. When he recuperated from the bladder-removal surgery, he was back out on the streets doing what he knew best — hustling, even though he was nearly seventy-four years old. On more than a couple of occasions, I remember stopping by his apartment to check on him and he was nowhere to be found. I was happy with the fact that he was moving ahead with his life. At times, I would stop by "the corner" to say hello to him, and the guys from the corner barbershop would ask, "You looking for the old man? He's around the corner — I'll get him."

True to the doctors' prediction, the cancer was back in three years, and with a vengeance. His oncologist recommended chemotherapy, but initially he did not want it because of what he witnessed with many of his friends who had undergone the treatment. When he asked my opinion, I told him that the decision had to be his. Even though I hoped and prayed that he would elect not to undergo chemotherapy, he decided to give it a try.

I vividly remember visiting Daddy one Sunday afternoon at his apartment. He told me that he decided to undergo chemotherapy because the

Taking Care of Daddy

doctors believed that it was the only way to kill the cancer cells that had metastasized. I felt faint, but I struggled not to show my fear. While we were talking, he pulled up his left pants leg to show me how his leg had swelled to twice its normal size. To make light of the situation, I said, "Your legs are mighty pretty with a little weight on them." We both laughed — anything to ease the tension of his condition.

As I feared, the chemotherapy treatments made Daddy violently sick, and he was unable to do anything for himself. On a Saturday morning, I got a call from Miss Maye, who said that Daddy had taken a turn for the worse. I got into my car, sped to his apartment in upper Northwest, raced upstairs to the second floor, and knocked on the door. When Miss Maye finally opened the door, I brushed her cheek with a kiss and made a mad dash into Daddy's bedroom. I took one look at him and called 911. Before the ambulance arrived, he stumbled into the bathroom, fell to his knees, and began vomiting. "Baby, I'm so sick," he said. The paramedics arrived and stood over Daddy while he remained on his knees, holding onto the toilet for dear life — vomiting and spilling his insides into that piece of cold porcelain with no end in sight. I was crying from the pit of my stomach.

From my soul and deep within my heart, I felt the kind of pain that only comes from seeing someone you love suffer, knowing that there is nothing you can do about it. It's the kind of pain you feel when a "life connection" is being broken. I would have welcomed the chance for the ground I stood on to open up and swallow me alive if it would help me escape seeing my daddy on his knees suffering — watching his insides gushing out like Niagara Falls, hearing him cry out, "Oh Lord! Oh Lord! Oh Lord!" I prayed just as hard as I could. I begged God to give me the strength to endure — the strength Daddy no longer had.

My father was readmitted to Howard University Hospital, a place that had become quite familiar to us within the past few years. The doctors administered medication to make him comfortable. That is all they could do. I did not bother to ask him, I had to tell him that he had to come live with me. I was the only one to take care of him. He looked at me and said, "Baby, I never thought you would want to take care of me."

Shocked, I looked at him and asked, "If not me, then who, Daddy?"

It hurt me to my heart to close down Daddy's apartment. It had been his home for more than thirty years and I knew he would not see it again. I hurt for the both of us because that small apartment held memories we had of our rare visits, including the one occasion we attempted to live under the same roof as father and daughter. That small one-bedroom apartment had been his home, his kingdom, his sanctuary, and his turf. As a salute to my father, I left the apartment as immaculate as he had kept it all of those years, right down to exterminating for roaches one last time. Because it was important to me that Daddy had some semblance of familiarity in his new home with me, I moved his bedroom set from his apartment into the downstairs bedroom of my duplex. I prepared as best I could to bring my father to his new home so that we could begin what was our final short journey together under the same roof.

Howard University Hospital assigned a social worker to help me obtain the equipment that was needed to care for a terminally ill patient. She was a middle-aged African American woman, short and plump, with a gentle voice and caring demeanor. She explained in detail the services Daddy was eligible to receive. Miss Maye stayed with me to help care for the precious love of her life for as long as she could. My father's second daughter, Brenda, and I had met approximately seven years before he became ill. She was pregnant with her second child, but would come by to lend a hand whenever she could.

Nights were the most difficult for Daddy because that was when his pain was worse. I would sit in his bedroom and listen to him reminisce about old times. He loved to talk about me when I was a baby. It tickled him when he told me stories about my funny behavior as a baby and little girl. According to him, I would not let anybody touch me or hold me except him and my mother. He said I was such a good little girl and it wasn't until I became a teenager that I got "messy." Finally, he told me that he had dreams of me becoming a politician — something I was not the least bit interested in doing. Brenda told me before Daddy did that he wanted me to become a politician — I don't know how he got that vision.

We held numerous conversations about life and men and he candidly answered my questions about how men think and why men behave the way that they do. He did not have many nice things to say about men and relationships with women, leaving me with the perception that men, in general, only wanted one thing from a woman — sex: Use her, and leave her. That was his environment — the hustler environment — the hustler mentality. But it was also becoming my reality.

He talked a lot about the agony of getting old, which he hated — calling old age "a disease" — and we also talked at length about life and death. During the short period that we lived together, Daddy revealed more about himself to me than at any other time in our lives. I learned so many things about my father from our late night conversations during his illness.

CHAPTER 23
Good-bye, Daddy

I was still trying to work as a freelance legal secretary, while simultaneously taking care of my father, paying Richard's tuition, and providing for myself as best as I could. It never failed that while on a work assignment I would receive that inevitable emergency call and would have to rush home to see about my father and Miss Maye. She did as much as she could, but she was growing weaker by the day from her own battle with colon cancer. As a result of this situation, job offers had begun to dry up. Then it came to a point when I could no longer work because my father required full-time care. His income consisted of a meager Social Security check, Supplemental Social Security check and food stamps — not nearly enough to cover expenses. Daddy had not worked a legal job in his life, and it bewildered me how he even got the Social Security benefits. The phone stopped ringing from law firms, and I was broke, scared, tired, and stressed beyond imagination.

While talking with Daddy one day, I gently questioned him about his insurance policy, a subject I quite frankly wanted to avoid. "I had to work for mine," he snapped, "you work for yours." My father was not only sick and penniless, but I would be the one left to pay his final expenses, a burden I could not afford.

I spent my days taking care of Daddy and Miss Maye — crying, worrying, and praying. One unforgettable evening, while my godmother and I were sitting alone in my living room, she calmly told me that she "had to go." She told me that my father was afraid to die and that she had to go before him because she wanted to be in heaven waiting when he arrived so that he wouldn't be afraid. Miss Maye had the strongest faith in God that I have ever witnessed.

The next morning, her son came to my apartment to take my precious godmother to live with her daughter, Nyman, a Muslim, and her family, in New Jersey. Within days, Daddy had to be readmitted to Howard University Hospital. While he was in the hospital, I took that opportunity to pay my beloved godmother a visit.

When I arrived at Nyman's home, I quietly entered Miss Maye's second-floor bedroom. Though she was confined to a hospital bed and had wasted away to skin and bones, she smiled that same comforting smile that I had cherished since childhood. We talked briefly. Mostly, I listened. She told me it was time for her "to go home." She stressed just how much she loved me, and told me to always pray and hold onto my faith, and to never forget that God will not put more on me than I can bear. She reassured me that when Daddy reached heaven, she would be waiting for him. That's the deep love she had for my father. I am sure that he loved her as best as he could during their fifty-year relationship.

Miss Maye died two days after I visited with her. Nyman asked me to make the funeral arrangements because her mother was Baptist and she was Muslim. It was with honor and love that I made funeral arrangements for the sweetest woman in the world that I knew. She was loved for her unselfishness and willingness to help anyone that she could, and throngs of people attended her funeral. When I told Daddy that Miss Maye died, he held his head down looking at the hospital floor and said, "Poor Maye."

Shortly after Daddy was released from the hospital, he became extremely ill again. This time, I drove him to the hospital because he wanted to sit in the back seat of the car. On the ride to the hospital, I watched him through the rearview mirror. He was sitting up as straight as an arrow — proud and quiet, taking in the sights. He knew that this would be the last time he would see his old surroundings. Shortly after reaching the hospital and being admitted, Daddy suddenly had problems breathing. The doctor advised him that if he was not put on a respirator immediately, he would die within the hour. I asked my father what he

Good-bye, Daddy

wanted to do. He told me that he wanted to go on the respirator. He said, "They might find a cure tomorrow."

What I know is that if a cure became available, he planned to be one of the first beneficiaries. Daddy was hoping for a miracle that never came. To this day, I don't believe Daddy knew what it meant to be on a respirator. I believe that if he had understood exactly what it entailed, he would have elected to go to sleep peacefully.

Doctors and nurses entered Daddy's room and asked me to step out of the room while they hooked him up to the respirator. When I was permitted to return to his room, I was completely unprepared for what awaited me. Daddy was traumatized; his eyes screamed fear and horror. His hands were strapped down so that he could not remove the ghastly contraption — a tube was inserted down his throat and machines were everywhere. I screamed. Brenda, my half-sister, maintained her calm and quickly ushered me out of the room and down the hall, hoping to calm my hysteria. I could hear myself screaming, "That's not my daddy! That's not my daddy!" My chest felt like it was going to explode. People in the hallway were looking at me with pity, some stopping to try to console me, hold me, and pray for me. The doctors urged me to go home, but I could not leave my daddy alone when he was so petrified. I got myself together enough to go back into his room and sit with him.

I was back at my apartment when finally I fell into a much-needed sleep. Sometime during the early morning, the telephone rang, startling me, and I hesitantly answered. It was the hospital. "Your father suffered a cardiac arrest," the doctor said. "However, we were able to revive him." They needed to know whether to resuscitate him or let him go if it happened again. I did not have to think twice. I knew what Daddy would want. "Let him go," I quietly responded to the doctor. "Let him go in peace."

I arrived at the hospital early the next morning. I needed to be with my father. He had developed sepsis, a blood infection, and was swollen to the point of being unrecognizable. His once small head was spread across the entire pillow like a blob. His hands and arms looked like those of a giant Pillsbury dough boy — as if they were about to explode. Nothing about him resembled the father I knew. I sat with him, talked to him, and read his eyes — that's how we communicated.

A friend of mine, Beto, came by to visit him. He asked me, "When was the last time you ate?" I shrugged my shoulders. I honestly didn't remember. After spending a few minutes with Daddy, Beto told him that he was going to take me across the street for a bowl of soup. Daddy nodded his swollen head. We quickly walked across the street to a small restaurant and ordered soup but I could not eat because I had no appetite. I thanked Beto for coming to visit and told him I had to get back to the hospital. As I rounded the corner of the intensive care unit, I saw Daddy raise his swollen head searching for me. As soon as he saw me coming, he slowly laid his head back on the pillow. When I looked at him, I knew our time together was short. I sat in the chair beside Daddy's bed. There was something in his eyes that let me know he didn't want to leave because he was worried about me. I leaned over and placed my mouth next to his ear and whispered to him that I would be fine and it was okay for him to go home and that I loved him. I called Brenda to tell her that if she wanted to see Daddy before he transitioned, she needed to come right away.

The last time he was in the hospital, he told me that,through all of this, I had been a "soldier." That was all I needed to hear from him. Finally, I did something right and my father understood that I could never abandon him. "Would you like me to read the 23rd Psalm to you?" I asked him. He nodded. I crossed the room, picked up the Bible, returned to his beside, turned to the 23rd Psalm, and took his hand in mine. As I began to read, Daddy held my hand. Then I felt his grasp loosen. I looked down at him. His eyes were slowly closing — like he was dozing off. The monitor began its frantic alarm. Doctors and nurses rushed into the room. The doctor looked at me. "Let him go," I said, calmly.

Daddy died peacefully while holding my hand. After he was pronounced dead, the nurse told me I could stay with him for thirty minutes, and after that his body had to be moved. I sat quietly with my father. I pulled the sheet down from his body and actually witnessed it transform slowly back to its natural state. Brenda arrived just as I was watching my father's miraculous transformation. It was over. This experience taught me that death is an amazing phenomenon. It is absolutely true that when one dies, the spirit is set free.

My father had two funeral services, one in Washington, DC, and the other in South Carolina. He was laid to rest in a light-brown metallic casket, and was dressed in one of his prized black suits, white shirt, a colorful tie with a perfect Windsor knot, and gold cuff links. He looked like a million dollars. His old DC hustler friends arrived in Cadillacs, Mercedes Benzes, and Lincolns. It was one sight to behold — old gray-haired hustlers stepping out of their showboat cars wearing fedora hats, some strutting with canes into the funeral home. A few were dressed in expensive suits while others came in casual wear. At Daddy's funeral, I saw my son, now nineteen years old, shed tears for his grandfather. Unfortunately, I had become so engrossed with my own chaotic life that it wasn't until the funeral that I realized for the first time the strong bond that had developed between Daddy and my son. They had their own special moments.

My father's hustler friends helped me to pay for his funeral, but I had no money to pay for his burial. I was frantic. Then, out of nowhere, I thought to call the family funeral home in South Carolina to ask about the cost to bury him there. Timothy Gilmore, a childhood friend who took over his father's mortuary business after he died, told me that my father's plot had been paid for years ago by his parents. I thanked God for directing me to make that telephone call. I hurriedly made arrangements to have Daddy's body shipped to South Carolina, where we would have the second funeral. Most of Daddy's hometown friends had predeceased him, but the few who remained, as well as what little family we had left, were at the service. Daddy was buried beside his father, mother, and brother. His funeral was held at a funeral home in South Carolina. Small, intimate repasts were held in DC and South Carolina to celebrate Daddy's life. That is how he would have wanted it.

Tired, sad, grieving, homeless, and broke, I heard a soft whisper, "Job well done."

CHAPTER 24
A NEW JOB, A NEW LIFE

D
ue to total lack of funds, immediately after burying my father, I
moved into a friend's one-bedroom apartment. Robert Hodge
and I had met years ago at a popular dance spot that featured
"oldies but goodies." It was a place where baby boomers flooded the
dance floor to enjoy hand-dancing, a DC favorite. Robert and I fre-
quented the dance hall and became regular dance partners. When we met,
he had been divorced for thirteen years and was not in a relationship.
Robert's jovial personality and strong, steady support during my father's
final days bolstered my courage to ask him for a temporary place to live.
He was aware of what I had been through and my financial situation. He
was by my side from the time my father died until he was buried in South
Carolina. When I returned from South Carolina, I needed somewhere to
crash just long enough to recoup from caring for my father and get a job.
Although I could have asked my mother if I could live with her, I was
not psychologically ready or willing to subject myself to her and my
brother's foolishness. I needed peace, quiet, and support.

Nobody really knew the absolute truth about my situation. I was a pro
at camouflage. I was attractive, dressed immaculately, and carried myself
like I owned the world. But in reality, I was at rock-bottom and there
was no place I wanted to crash except at Robert's, and I asked him if I
could. I promised him that I would find an apartment as soon as I found
a job and saved a little money.

Within three months of Daddy's death, I landed a professional position at the national organization that recruited me as a secretary in 1969, and that I left in 1978 to pursue professional employment. As I promised Robert, I immediately began to look for an apartment. The Chapter 7 bankruptcy on my credit, however, made me nervous about submitting an application for any apartment, not to mention the quaint, two-bedroom unit in an upscale Silver Spring, Maryland, community that I desperately wanted. I remember driving through the community thinking that this beautiful and soothing atmosphere would be the perfect place for me to continue to heal. After driving through the apartment complex for a few days, I took a deep breath and went inside to look at a two-bedroom model apartment, which was absolutely beautiful. I called the resident manager the following day and requested an appointment with her. She set a time for the next day at 11 a.m.

When I arrived at her office, I politely introduced myself to Hillary Caswell, a white woman in her mid-thirties, who invited me into her office and offered me a cup of tea. We talked more about my financial situation and the criteria that she looked for when leasing an apartment. Needless to say, at that time the only positive criterion I could offer was a stable job. I explained my situation, and divulged the bankruptcy while highlighting my credentials and gainful employment. I asked matter-of-factly, though feeling jittery and somewhat intimidated, about the feasibility of my being approved for an apartment in her complex. She asked me to complete an application and leave a deposit — which I did — and she promised to call me the next day.

I hoped Hillary Caswell would live up to her promise to telephone me. Robert had been kind and patient throughout my stay, but I knew it was time to move on. He was ready to have his space back and I desperately needed my own space. I knew Robert had his fingers crossed for me.

The next day while at work, the telephone rang. It was Hillary Caswell. I held my breath, not knowing what to expect, but hoping for the best. "Hi, Ms. Chappelle, this is Hillary Caswell. I'm calling to give you your move-in date." I screamed out of pure unadulterated joy. I still remember her words to me: "Just continue to move forward; don't look back at the past." She also said that she was happy to give me a chance, and if I ran into any problems to let her know immediately. Thankfully, I did not run into any problems and enjoyed every minute in my new home. It truly was a healing sanctuary.

In the suburb of Silver Spring, Maryland, my life began anew in my beautiful, spacious, two-bedroom apartment with skylights, fireplace, large balcony with two entrances — one through the kitchen and one off of the living room. I could not remember when I felt so happy. Many times I sat on the floor in the middle of the empty living room floor and cried, thanking and praising God for giving me yet another chance to get it right. Slowly, piece-by-piece, I furnished the apartment, hung pictures, bought custom draperies — I was living in "apartment heaven."

In July 1995, Walter and I were divorced again. We still owned the house in Virginia Beach because he did not take my name off of the deed or the mortgage. He wanted to sell the property and I offered no objection. During our first divorce settlement, we agreed that the condo, which was lost in bankruptcy, was mine. The house in Virginia Beach was his. Yet, during our second divorce, Walter offered to give me a percentage from the sale of the house. When the sale was final, I received a check from him for the exact amount on which we agreed. Surprisingly, after a few weeks, Walter called to ask if he could come for a brief visit. He sounded serious and said he needed to talk to me, leaving me puzzled. I didn't know what was on his mind this time, but I knew I was not marrying him again.

He arrived late on a Friday evening. He did not mention anything about our divorce. He asked how I was doing, about work, and engaged in general conversation, chatting the way we used to until the wee hours of the morning. He finally told me the truth about what happened to our first marriage. The reason he would not be intimate with me during our first marriage while he was in stationed in New Orleans was because he was sleeping with multiple women — five that he mentioned or remembered. I was outdone. I suspected that it was another woman, but a harem — I was blown away. Thank God he didn't touch me after that!

When it was time to retire for the night, Walter slept in the guest bedroom alone, and I slept in my bedroom alone — just like in the beginning. The next morning, he wanted to take me shopping to get what I needed for my new apartment. When we returned, he helped me pot a few plants with his usual libation close by.

The reason for his visit was to assure himself that I was doing fine, perhaps because of his guilty feelings about the manner in which he sought the divorce. Actually, he did not need to feel guilty about anything because he gave me what no man ever did — guaranteed security. He hung in there through my illness and provided me with medical coverage for ten years. I know if I searched the four corners of the world, I could never find a better friend than Chief Petty Officer Walter Pugh. On Sunday morning, we had our final breakfast together — scrambled eggs, fried potatoes, bacon, hot rolls, and mimosas. After breakfast, he prepared to leave for Louisiana where he was still stationed. I walked him to the door where, we lovingly embraced, like old friends. I heard him descending the steps leading to the parking lot. When I could no longer hear him on the steps, I went onto the balcony, where I watched my special friend get into his car and drive out of my complex.

Suddenly, it made sense when Walter said he had sent the divorce papers by mail instead of just telling me straight out because he "didn't want to hurt me." Watching him leave hurt worse than I ever imagined it could. Our embrace at the door said it all for both of us: Good-bye, my dear friend; it's time for us to move forward with our respective lives. I silently wished him well as my heart literally ached. Not to my surprise, our special friendship continues to this day.

A New Job, A New Life

CHAPTER 25

THE MONEY PIT

I n 1996, I bought a near-dilapidated rowhouse in Northeast Washington on Capitol Hill, and lived through the horror of its six-year renovation. The old adage "you do what you have to do" is real.

I met Solomon Hughes, a contractor, while searching for someone to renovate my newly purchased Capitol Hill home. After meeting and interviewing a number of contractors, I hired his company to renovate my rowhouse. We spent many hours going over renovation plans for the house. He began to do the renovations on the house but, after awhile, I became concerned because he had not presented a bill to me for the work he had done. I asked him repeatedly about the bill but he insisted that I not worry about it — that he would get the bill to me. When I demanded that he give me an invoice because I did not want an unexpectedly gigantic bill all at one time, surprisingly, he calmly told me that he was very taken with me, not to worry about it, and that he would bill me in increments. I remember like it was yesterday when he said to me, "I can't afford to buy you a new house, but I can build you one." I was overwhelmed. It was the first time anyone outside of Walter Pugh offered to do anything of that magnitude for me. He was not my type — he was stout and suffered from occasional bleeding from his rectum, and advanced gingivitis, which caused bad breath, and he had a generous stomach. I was not physically attracted to him even thoug he was fifteen years younger than me, so I knew that our union would not be for a lifetime. While I preferred younger men, I was always uncomfortable with the large difference in our ages. However, we made a pact. While Solomon was a tremendously skilled home renovation expert, he had neglected to get a license, insurance, and bonding for his business. We agreed that he would renovate my home (I would buy the material) and I would do the paperwork to get him licensed, bonded, and insured.

After a few months, he moved in with me and I grew to care a great deal for him. I was not in love with him, but I was content for awhile. I saw to it that he got his gums treated, joined a gym, and practiced healthy eating. I also encouraged him to see a proctologist, a medical doctor specializing in rectal disorders. After much pressure from me, he saw the specialist and learned that he had two huge bleeding hemorrhoids that needed to be surgically removed. He underwent the surgery successfully and to my knowledge had no more incidents of rectal bleeding.

After helping him become licensed, bonded, and insured, I completed an application for him to become a minority contractor in the District of Columbia, where he was able to work alongside the "big boys." He had a knack for making money and, for once in a long time, I enjoyed not having to worry about finances. We did whatever we wanted to do. We traveled extensively, ate out often at fine restaurants, bought whatever we wanted, and enjoyed life.

There was, however, one huge problem. I kept my part of the bargain whereby Solomon became licensed, bonded, and insured. However, Solomon began to slow down dramatically on completing renovations on my house. His thinking, to my surprise, was that if he completed the renovations on my home, I would ask him to leave. In my mind that was absolutely ludicrous. He even argued with me that I should put his name on the deed because of the work he had put into the house thus far, although the house was still in a mess and I was buying the material. There was no way on this earth that his name or anyone's name other than mine was going to be on the deed. I thought, "He must have fallen and bumped his head." Here I go again, I said to myself.

We began to have serious problems — nobody is perfect, but he had a mean, selfish streak. He quickly became totally unappealing to me because the quickest way for me to lose interest in a man is for him to take my kindness for weakness. I was extremely resentful that I kept my part of the agreement to help him build his company, but he did not honor his part to complete the renovations on my house. I was livid! To top it off, he was a hypocrite — a Jehovah's Witness who supposedly did not believe in holidays like Thanksgiving and Christmas.

Solomon was a big man, actually on the plump side, even though he was in strict denial about that. He enjoyed my cooking immensely and loved to eat. To get over the conflict of enjoying the holiday feasts that I would prepare, he would call holidays by different names. For example, Thanksgiving became "Turkey Day." Whatever he called it, he enjoyed the hefty plates of food. It's amazing how men can change the order of things to fit their needs ("man law").

During the six-year renovation of my house, I lived through the gutting of the entire house, which caused enormous amounts of dust and dirt. I already suffered from allergies but these pollutants caused chronic sinus infections and respiratory problems. There was a time during the renovation when the upstairs toilet was temporarily placed in the middle of the upstairs bedroom area with no walls until he got around to building a temporary enclosure. Twice I had to be rushed to my ophthalmologist because of the dirt and dust that caused the tear ducts in my eyes to completely close, requiring a minor surgical procedure to open them. It was not long after that incident that I became sick of Solomon — angry with having to exist in squalor because of his fear that I would put him out if he completed the renovations as promised. The day I left on a business trip to Chicago, I told him to be out of my house by the time I returned. I'd had enough! To my chagrin, he was still in my house when I returned home. It turned to be was a good thing that he had not left at that point, because I was about to experience another nightmare.

CHAPTER 26
GOOD-BYE, MA

Our family, what few were left, came together Thanksgiving 1998 to be with my mother, who was dying from lung cancer and barely aware of the world around her. The pain medication administered to her made her close to comatose — eyes half-open, slightly snoring, and rapidly slipping away from us. It was devastating for me to see my mother, an extremely proud woman, deteriorate into virtually a vegetative state — helpless and dependent, something she detested. Five years after my father's death, it was happening all over again — except this time it was my mother. I did not want to watch my mother suffer. I knew from experience that I was unable to do anything to help her pain. The only thing I could do was to pray and be with her.

It all started when my mother continually complained of a sore throat. Her doctor diagnosed her as having sinus infections. At first I had no reason to think otherwise; however, after perpetual sore throats, weight loss, and fatigue, I became concerned. Although she never had a big appetite, she lost all desire to eat. I insisted that she see a specialist, but being her stubborn self, she agreed with her incompetent doctor that she had sinusitis. My mother can be quite snappy, but this time her biting attitude did not dissuade me from insisting on a specialist. After much cajoling, I made an appointment for her at Georgetown University Hospital. Shortly after her second appointment, she was diagnosed with lung cancer. Although my mother had been a chain smoker for many years, she had quit that nasty habit several years earlier, but obviously several years too late.

Similar to the treatment for my father's illness, her oncologist recommended radiation and then chemotherapy. In the past she steadfastly said she would not take chemotherapy treatments if she ever had cancer, but like my father, she wanted to live, so she decided to take the treatments. I stayed close by because of the side effects of the treatments. Her first radiation treatment was uneventful, but the second treatment made her so violently ill that she could not talk or move her head. The radiation treatments caused her throat to become so sore that she was admitted to the hospital. Because of the severe side effects of the radiation, this therapy was stopped immediately.

My mother then agreed to try the chemotherapy, but I knew what to expect, and cannot describe my angst. I was certain I could not handle another ordeal like the one I struggled through five years earlier. She handled the first chemotherapy treatment with few complications, which gave me some relief and I began to think that perhaps she was one of the few who could tolerate it and get better. However, the second treatment left her desperately ill, and her doctors recommended that no further treatments be administered. There came a point when there was nothing the doctors could do for my mother, who had become withdrawn and emaciated. It was not long before she was placed under home hospice care to control her pain.

After having watched my father valiantly fight his bladder cancer, I was not in denial about what was about to happen. As determined as she had always been, I knew my mother would not win this fight and it ripped apart my insides. Before she became bedridden, I tried to talk to her about our relationship, but she was not amenable in the least. Her response to me was, "You are crazy." I had no choice but to begin to prepare for the inevitable. I would have to learn how to live without bringing closure to the rift between my mother and me.

I have heard people and ministers say over and over again to adults who complain about their experiences with their parent(s) to "get over it." I have always thought that was the most asinine and insensitive thing anybody could say without experiencing the hurt of not having the unconditional love of a parent. The sensible thing to say would be "learn to live with it" because it is something one never gets over. I had no choice but to finally accept that I would not hear her tell me that she loved me. She was leaving and there was nothing I could do about it. At least my father told me that I had been a soldier — that was good enough. My mother was never good with admitting anything — everybody was crazy or lying. My heart would not be mended as I hoped it would, and while I might not be whole, I was determined to learn to live with it.

While family and friends enjoyed the Thanksgiving dinner feast at Ma's house, I was upstairs attempting to give her water through a straw. I gently lifted her head from her pillow so that she would take a sip, but she was too weak to pull the water through the straw. I laid her head gently back onto the pillow. Our eyes locked — her eyes spoke volumes. Her eyes said, "I'm ready to go. Let me go." My father's death and now my mother's impending death were almost too much for me to bear. Solomon, with his ongoing support, was my rock during this period. His strong arms were there to hold me and his broad shoulders there to cry on after every pain-filled visit with my mother. I needed to hold onto every moment with her. It was imperative for me to know that I did all I could for her as I had always done. I wanted to know what she needed, to read her eyes. I had learned five years ago to communicate visually.

When I arrived at my mother's home to take care of her on the morning of December 27, 1998, I took one look at her and I knew it was time to call her hospice nurse to have her admitted into the hospice facility. The time for her transition was near. Her hospice nurse, an angel from Jamaica, quickly came and examined her and called for transport. She then called the hospice facility and I heard her say, "I'm bringing Mrs. Spelman in." It was not long before the ambulance arrived to take my mother to a hospice facility in upper Northwest DC. Two female ambulance attendants handled my mother with loving care and concern, gently placing her on the gurney and expertly rolling her out of her home of 32 years. Shauney, my mother's favorite grandchild, began screaming for her as she was being taken out of the house. Thrift tried to calm her down by telling her that they were driving to the hospital right away to see her and not to cry. I rode in the ambulance, listening to my mother speak in a language unknown to man.

It was not the first time I experienced this phenomenon; it happened with my father before he was put on the respirator. I heard that, shortly before a person dies, he or she will talk in an unknown language to an invisible someone or spirit whose presence is only known by the person making the transition. In my mind, I thought it was an angel waiting to escort my mother through the pearly gates. I watched and listened intently and suddenly realized that she was talking to God — it was a private conversation. When we arrived at the hospice facility, the staff lovingly whisked her away to make her comfortable.

I waited in the lounge area, as the nurse instructed, until they got my mother settled in her room. The hospice facility offered a world of love and peace for those making their final transition. When I was told that I could see my mother, I walked into her room and noticed that the scarf she insisted on wearing to cover her baldness from the chemo had been removed. After a soothing bath, she was lying there like a newborn baby — completely bald — but she was alert and her skin was glistening. Her room had soothing music piped in and there was a breathtaking view of plush green rolling hills that could be seen through a huge picture window. As I sat down beside her bed, Thrift and Shauney entered the room. Shauney visibly began to relax once she experienced the pleasant ambience of the room, and saw that her grandmother was once again alert. My mother could not talk to us, but she could focus on our faces and I believe she could hear us.

The nurse informed me that hospice center rules allowed family members to prepare meals for their visitors. I decided to rush home and prepare a few appetizers so that my mother's visitors could eat and keep her company as long as they desired. Leaning in close, I told her that I would be back in a flash with food for her guests. As I was about to leave, my mother, weak and fragile and on the threshold of death, miraculously raised her cancer-ravaged body and gazed at me like never before. She stared deeply and intently into my eyes for what seemed like minutes before lying back on the bed. The whites of her eyes had turned gray — the light of life was gone. To this day, I still wonder what her eyes were trying to tell me. I believe she was telling me that she loved me. I hope so, because I loved her.

Good-bye, Ma

As soon as I arrived home and was beginning to put together the food for guests, the telephone rang. When I answered, it was Thrift. "She's gone," he said.

I spun around in a state of shock before I got the presence of mind to call Solomon to tell him what happened. I then drove as fast as I could back to the hospice center. The nurse who cared for my mother during her final days was sitting in a chair in her room, which was now dimly lit. When I walked in, her nurse told me that my mother had a beautiful transition. She lay perfectly still, her eyes closed, her face blanketed in the kind of peace that surpasses all human understanding. My mother did not fight death. She accepted death as part of life. I sat in a chair at the foot of her bed in front of the window overlooking the beautiful, lush, rolling hills.

I turned my attention to my mother and stared at the corpse of the woman who birthed me — who gave me life. She looked long and thin lying in that bed — stiff, no longer suffering — just gone. I sat there with her for a while. Both parents were gone now. I was trying to cope with emotions that, to this day, I still cannot describe. Even though we never had the relationship I craved, she was still my mother and I loved her.

In that instant, I remembered the last conversation we had about death. I had taken her to her doctor's appointment. When we got home and before we got out of the car, I asked, "Are you scared?"

"No," she said softly. "I'm not scared, but I do hate to leave the people who care about me."

Before leaving my mother at the hospice center, I prayed to God to give her peace and to welcome her into his kingdom. I also asked Him to give me the strength to go on. The last words I said to her before leaving her room were, "Ma, I did the best I could." As I left her room, I said, "God bless you."

During the funeral, I thanked Reggie for coming. He was my first husband and was there to say good-bye to my mother, who was his friend. Though my marriage to Reggie was turbulent, to say the least, he and my mother maintained a strong friendship and he was visibly distressed that she was gone. He was there with his longtime friend, Gerald Cole, and we all exchanged pleasantries. Solomon was one of the pallbearers. He had been with me throughout my mother's illness, helping me handle the pain, agony, and disbelief of how cancer ravages the human body. To witness firsthand the agony of a terminally ill parent is a gut-wrenching experience. There is absolutely nothing anybody can do but pray to God for relief, and finally plead with Him to bring them home to end the suffering. To live through that horror with both parents, for me, was more than devastating. That experience is another testimony that God will put no more on us than we can bear — it only makes us stronger and more humble.

At my mother's funeral, Reverend Gerard spoke eloquently and kindly about my mother and her family — Toby and Thrift. He continually praised the virtues of Sister Spelman, Deacon Spelman, and Toby. Not once did he mention that my mother had a daughter, or show the courtesy of uttering my name. In a moment of overwhelming grief and anger, I blurted out in church, "She had a daughter, too!" Thrift, who was sitting one row in front of me, turned and said, "Ssshhh."

"Don't you tell me to be quiet," I angrily retorted. Besides, Thrift was the last person whose opinion I cared about.

We buried my mother in the cemetery next to her brothers and sisters. It took every ounce of strength for me to leave my mother in a box on that frigid day in January 1999. "God, I can't take it," I cried in Solomon's arms.

Months later, my mother's Last Will and Testament was provided to me by Thrift. I was mentioned twice. I was bequeathed a set of china and one-half of her house, which was left to me and Toby. My mother gave Thrift a life estate tenancy so that he would have a place to live until he died. But in a matter of a few short years, her will would be a source of betrayal and disrespect of her wishes.

After my mother died, Solomon began to have affairs. Finally, with some reluctance, he left. I was hurt, lonely, and scared of being alone again. I decided I wanted to be married; the dating thing just was not getting it for me.

CHAPTER 27
MEET FRANKLIN CARTER

In the early 1980s, Franklin and I met through an acquaintance during my abusive marriage to Derrick Frye, shortly before I left him for good. Margaret Sheffield, a relative, was planning to set up house with Franklin, who had recently been released from prison. What little I knew about Franklin was what I learned from Margaret and the family gossip about their relationship. Supposedly, he was the man she had secretly spent years visiting in prison and fell hard for. She was a heavy-set, dark-brown-skinned woman and Franklin was relatively tall and thin. They looked much like the "odd couple." Margaret was average-looking with beautiful black hair. She wore glasses; had a large, high rear end; and heavy, hairy legs that some men considered sexy. She, too, had her share of abusive relationships.

It was not long before Margaret brought Franklin to visit with me and Derrick. He was very quiet, as a matter of fact, unnaturally quiet and most unattractive. He was one of the most unattractive men I ever met. In fact, there was nothing appealing about him except for his voice — he spoke with a deep, Barry White-like voice. When he finally engaged in conversation with us, I found him to be surprisingly intelligent. Within a year of Margaret and Franklin living together, she confided in me that there were problems in paradise. By this time, Derrick and I were on the verge of a divorce. According to Margaret, Franklin was back in his life of crime, and I would later find out that she was his willing accomplice. It was alleged that he was embezzling large sums of money from his employer — embezzling by day and dealing drugs by night. It was alleged that Margaret was his co-conspirator in the embezzlement scheme. As is customary with men like Franklin, he grew tired of Margaret after he had no more use for her and was ready to move on to "greener pastures." His abandonment outraged her to the point that she became bitter and extremely vindictive. She did not care who she hurt as long as she destroyed Franklin Carter. If she could not have him, nobody could — she was obsessed with him. During this fiasco, she confided in her brother-in-law, a drug enforcement official, about the embezzlement scheme and her involvement. In turn, he notified the FBI and referred her to an attorney to try to work a deal for her testimony against Franklin. As a result, he was placed under surveillance and later arrested for embezzlement while Margaret, in turn, received total immunity for her part in the crime.

I was working for a law firm when, one morning, I received a surprise call from Franklin. I was shocked to hear from him because I didn't know him well at all. The purpose of his phone call was to find out what I had heard about his case — what Margaret was saying about it. I told him that I didn't know anything much about it. After that call, he began to call me at my office regularly to talk. There was no question in his mind that he was facing a stiff prison sentence. He often told me he was comfortable talking to me because I listened to him and didn't pass judgment on him, but he was also consumed with the reality that it was just a matter of time before he would lose his freedom again. His voice was intriguing and I was caught off-guard by his fake intelligence. I made the decision to spend time with him — to fill my empty space.

Within two months, he was sentenced to a lengthy prison term and was sent to Lewisburg Federal Penitentiary in Pennsylvania. Except for visiting my brother, it was my policy not to visit men in prison. I visited Franklin once in Lewisburg, and from that experience I knew that I would never return to such a dreary, inhumane, cold, animalistic environment. I knew for a fact that I had no interest in being involved with a man who chose a life of crime. As far as I could see, it was a life where people existed like slaves living in a cage — told when to eat, bathe, go to the bathroom — a life that was seemingly normal to him, but unfathomable to me. I remember him once telling me that what was unnatural on the street was natural in prison. I never forgot that.

Soon after I returned home from my first and last visit with him in prison, I changed my telephone number, refused his prison telephone calls, and went on with my life. It would be years before I would hear from him again. But still unbeknownst to me, I had already opened the door to the beginning of my worst nightmare.

* * *

In the summer of 1986, I was visiting with my family at Aunt Eunice's house in Washington, DC, while recuperating from my first surgery in Portsmouth, Virginia. While there, the telephone rang. Aunt Eunice answered it and to my astonishment told me that the phone call was for me. I was confused because I could not imagine who would be calling me at her house. I hesitantly took the phone from my aunt and said, "Hello." A woman's voice was on the line. It was Carrie, Franklin's sister, saying that she was calling for him and asking me to hold on. I was more than dumbfounded. He had served four years in prison for embezzlement. Franklin came on the line with his deep hypnotizing voice and said, "Hello." He told me that he had been trying to locate me ever since he had been released from prison. I asked him how he found me at my aunt's house, and he replied that he went through all the people in the phone book with my last name and began calling the numbers listed and luckily he found me at my aunt's number. I told him I was married and living in Virginia Beach. He told me he was in a halfway house and would be released soon. He asked to see me before I left to go back to Virginia Beach. I was curious enough to agree to see him, but didn't know what to expect.

I visited him a few days later at the halfway house before returning to Virginia Beach. He seemed taller than I remembered and we talked a long time about the past and his plans for the future. According to Franklin, he would definitely not go back to prison. I really didn't care whether or not he went back to prison, because my mind was on the second surgery that I was facing.

Franklin contacted me again after the surgery and when Walter was deployed to sea on the USS Kennedy, an aircraft carrier. I found out that he was working with a full-service insurance and brokerage firm in Bethesda, Maryland. What amazed me about him was his ability to get good jobs with his background. However, I figured out that his charisma, intellect, and rhetoric misled many people so I imagined that it was easy for him to "get over" on folks. He could have easily become a millionaire simply by using his voice, but that would have been too much like right. His narcissistic mantra was that he had "the voice to make women moist."

We began to talk again. At that time, he drove a baby-blue Cadillac Seville with a phone installed in it during a time when only executives or hustlers had car phones. Over a short period of time, I suspected that he was back in the life, doing what he did best — hustling, conning, conniving, and lying. I remember vividly the night he was determined to play mind games with me to see how far he could push my buttons before I crashed. After I got tired of his game, I faked a cry — he bought my con and he was satisfied because he believed he had triumphed over me — silly fool. That was always his ultimate goal — to control and conquer. What he didn't know was that I "faked" a cry to see how he handled that. This is when I figured out his game for sure! If only he knew that he did not win then nor would he win in the future. After all, I was Never Duncan's daughter and that was the end of that, so I thought.

A few months later, Franklin called to tell me that to tell me that he had been very ill and was hospitalized after eating tainted canned smoked oysters. I recalled that he loved canned smoked oysters and ate them often. He asked if he could come by the condo to visit for just a short while. I said yes, but emphasized that he could come by for a short while only because I had something planned. There were no plans, but I was not interested in spending any significant time with him. He arrived at my condo and we talked about his health and held a general conversation. Before he left, he asked for a glass of water and I complied. I gave him a glass of ice water and watched him sip it while we talked. He did not stay long as agreed. I told him to take care of himself and wished him well. When he left, I immediately took the glass that he drank from and threw it in the trash. No telling what disease he had!

A year passed before I received another telephone call I from Franklin. This time he told me that he had a baby girl, Latisha. I congratulated him, but I could not fathom him being anybody's father — especially the father of a female child. When I asked him what made him call me to tell me about the baby, he sounded surprised and replied, "I want you to know everything about my life." I was quite perplexed about his reply. As a matter of fact, I didn't give a rat's ass about what he did with his life and I would tell him that on many future occasions.

While working for the insurace and brokerage firm, Franklin committed another embezzlement crime that would send him back to federal prison for eleven years at the age of thirty. I would not see or hear from him for fifteen years. My mother died on December 28, 1998, and he was released from prison on December 28, 1999. During the years that Franklin was absent, many things transpired in my life. My son graduated from college; Walter and I divorced twice; I experienced poverty and filed Chapter 7 bankruptcy; my godmother, father and mother died of cancer; and I lived with a male acquaintance for four months until I found work and was able to rent an apartment.

* * *

After my mother's death, I applied to study for a doctor of education degree with a minor in political science in 2000 at a university in Washington, DC. After studying education for one year with political science as my minor, I decided to work toward a doctor of philosophy degree instead of a doctor of education degree. The Ph.D. would allow more flexibility in endeavors outside of education, such as consulting, writing, lecturing, research, or teaching at the university level. I was busy with the program of study and doing extremely well. The doctoral program kept my mind occupied and I found it to be intellectually challenging. I was pursuing my lifelong dream of earning a doctorate. I would be the first in my family to receive a Ph.D., and wanted to leave my educational accomplishments as a legacy for the young people in my family. Just when I was in the middle of my program, though, something evil was lurking in the shadows, in the dark — quiet, scheming, ready for his next prey.

After serving eleven years in prison, Franklin was released back into the community. My half-sister, Brenda, telephoned me on four occasions within four years after he was back on the streets to tell me that Franklin contacted her and desperately wanted me to call him. I told her, "Hell no, I don't want to talk to him." But Satan knows just when to strike. I was moving along fine with my life and my studies, but I was lonely. Again, I felt incomplete without a man in my life. Ironically, I had material possessions that many women dreamed about — a lovely renovated home on Capitol Hill, a Jaguar, and an SUV. I lived my life as I saw fit, went wherever I wanted to go, and should have been secure enough in myself to wait for the right man. Better still, I should have been satisfied being by myself.

Brenda telephoned me one day and told me that Franklin had called her again. She talked to me about how depressed he was because of problems he was having with his daughter. The kicker was when she said, "People do change — you are no better than anybody else."

Franklin was working as a patient coordinator in a cancer center of a major hospital in DC. He had a decent job and I remember asking myself, "How does he always get decent jobs with his record?" I thought about what my sister said about people changing and decided to take his telephone number at work and give him a call. What the hell — just a telephone call. Why not? I nervously dialed the telephone number that Brenda had given me and lo and behold, that familiar deep, sexy, penetrating voice answered, "Good afternoon, Franklin speaking." I said, "Hi Franklin." He sounded surprised and asked how I was doing. I replied that I was doing very well. The second question was, "Are you married?" I replied, "No." He asked, "Why not?" I responded, "Because I don't want to be." He then asked to take me to dinner. I thought to myself, now this is strange — Franklin asking to take me to dinner.

That was a first. Taking a woman out to dinner was not his style. Maybe he has changed, as my half-sister said. I told him I would think about the dinner proposition and get back to him.

We had dinner approximately two weeks later. We decided to meet in downtown DC — he was in his Lincoln Continental and I was in my Jaguar, looking chic in a full-length fur coat. We were talking on our cell phones as I was driving to meet him because I wanted a description of his car, so I could identify it when I approached him. I eyeballed the car based on the description he provided. He had pulled over waiting for me with his blinkers flashing. I pulled directly in front of him. He hurriedly got out of his car and approached me on the passenger side. I unlocked the door and he slid in.

We looked at each other — I don't know what he was thinking, but I noticed how ugly and brown his teeth were. I surmised that he was still heavily smoking. His hair was completely different than I remembered. In the past, his hair was natural and cut at a medium length. Now his hair was extremely wavy, jet-black — like a chemical was being used. In my mind I wondered, "What did he do to his hair and why?" It didn't seem like his style. I would later find out that he dyed his hair jet-black and kept it cut short to show his hair's natural wave pattern. We decided to eat at a well-known seafood restaurant in Southwest. I followed him as we drove our separate cars to the restaurant. We parked on the restaurant's parking lot and went inside. We were seated promptly, but I was rather uncomfortable and he seemed uncomfortable as well. It had been fifteen years since we had any contact with each other. To ease his discomfort, he immediately ordered a double Courvoisier and I ordered my usual margarita, with no salt, on the rocks. For a while we held a general conversation. It was not long before he started in on his rhetorical foolishness: "I am a man of truth. There are no gray areas, only truth," he said. I replied that there are always gray areas — situations and circumstances sometimes dictate the necessity for flexibility. He vehemently disagreed with me and began throwing around names of philosophers such as Khalil Gibran!

The truth of the matter is that Franklin wouldn't know truth if someone poured it down his throat. Another insane moment at the restaurant was when he told me that, while on the inside, he made a commitment to himself that he would be with only one woman at a time. His "ho" days were over. He proudly announced to me that he did not go to movies, he didn't dance, he disliked clubs, and he did not travel. He said that after being in the military, he had already seen the world. I realized that his only comfort level was in the dreary ghetto streets with men and women who stayed high, drunk, or both — people who had nothing substantial going on in their lives. I drank my margarita and rolled my eyes up to the sky saying to myself, "Who does he think he is talking to?" He began to talk about his disdain for Peggy, the woman he was currently living with and who he had the audacity to refer to as "ghetto fabulous," when ghetto is all he knew.

I watched him order one double Courvoisier after another and finally asked him when he started drinking alcohol. When we spent time together before, he did not drink liquor. Many years ago when he decided to stop using cocaine, he abruptly stopped — cold turkey. I came to understand that, when one addiction is abandoned, another immediately takes its place. He told me that Peggy was a heavy Jack Daniels drinker, and because of that, he began to drink also — always the victim, never taking responsibility for his own screw-ups. It was always somebody else's fault.

What I wanted to know, and what I asked him, was: (1) What are you doing to make money other than your job? and (2) Why was it important to talk to me? To the first question, he responded that he was not involved in anything illegal, that he was living solely on his paycheck, but that it was extremely difficult because he was accustomed to hustling and having large sums of money. To my second question he responded, "I need you." The last answer bothered me, and I asked him what "needing me" meant. All he would say about that is, "I just need you — I've always loved you and always will." When the waiter came over to take our orders, Franklin insisted that I order for him. I told him I was not going to order for him and that he should order for himself. He insisted, so I reluctantly ordered his meal. I reminded myself that it was only dinner and only one night. I did not take him seriously at all. After we ate dinner and he paid the bill with his debit card, he asked me to leave the tip because he did not carry cash. I shook my head, left the tip, and prepared to leave the restaurant. Luckily, we did not have to pay to park our cars; otherwise, he would have been "short."

We agreed that he would follow me home to make sure that I arrived safely. I found a parking space a short walk from my house. He found one behind me and walked me home. Being courteous, I invited him in. We sat at my high, round, multi-colored table inside a nook next to my living room in front of a window facing the street. He asked for a drink and I told him to help himself. I was astonished at how much he drank — he was steadily pouring liquor. I finally told him how surprised I was that he drank liquor because his father was an alcoholic and died a terrible death as a result of his alcoholism. I remember Franklin saying he would never drink because of how his father died. Thankfully, he did not stay long. As I walked him to the door, he gently kissed me on the cheek, and we said goodnight. I closed and locked the door and went up to bed asking myself, "What in the hell is going on with him and this liquor thing?"

The following morning, Saturday, I awoke to a steady snow. I realized that I needed to get to the grocery store, as the forecast indicated a large snowstorm was on the way. Shortly after I got out of bed, Franklin called. He asked what I was doing and I told him I was on my way to the grocery store. He suggested that he drive me, because it was beginning to snow hard. I hesitated, but then agreed. When he arrived at my home a half-hour later, wearing a pair of jeans and a black skull cap on his head, he looked like a bona fide middle-aged thug. I was not prepared for his ghetto cap, but, well, that was on him —he was not my man. He drove me to Shoppers Food Warehouse in Virginia to buy groceries. After leaving Shoppers, and on the way back to my house with the groceries, Franklin was playing a CD by Jaheim, a well-known artist who refers to himself as a "thug balladeer," who has a unique voice and makes mesmerizing music. Even though I could not decipher Jaheim's jargon, his music did have an appeal and, of course, Franklin knew the words to the entire CD. Once home, he told me not to try to take the bags in — he would do that because he did not want me to fall because the snow was steadily falling. First feather in his cap! Once the bags were in the house, he hung around for awhile and of course he needed to have a drink. I thanked him for driving me to the store. After he left, I went about putting the groceries away and doing my weekend chores.

Franklin began to call me daily and usually asked to drop by. He was careful not to involve sex in his scheme to get with me. He was still living with Peggy and his plan was to convince me that he was faithful to one woman at a time. After awhile, I noticed that he began to frequently express his desire to end the relationship with her. I strongly suggested to him that he try something that he had never done before — rent an apartment and live alone. I urged him to give himself time to sort out his life. My perpetual questions to him were: Why was it necessary to live with a woman all the time? Why couldn't you live alone until you found the right relationship? But, he had an excuse for everything — his salary was too low and he could not afford to rent an apartment. I suggested he find a roommate but that was too easy. There was always a reason why he could not rent an apartment or live alone.

When a highly acclaimed play about men on the "down low" came to the city, I wanted to see it. I telephoned Franklin and asked if he would accompany me to the play. I was surprised that he said yes, since he was a man who said he was uncomfortable in theaters because of the darkness and the inability to see what's going on — always afraid someone was after him, his past perpetually haunting him. The play was at 7:30 p.m. on a weekday. We agreed to meet at the Warner Theater at 7:15 p.m. I was quite nervous about going to the play with him because I had no idea as to how he would behave because I didn't have that type of experience with him. Lord please, not that ugly ghetto black skull cap. If he wore that, we would not be attending the play together and that was that. He was the only guy I knew to ask. I was not involved with anyone at that time and the men that I knew were married. There is nothing worse for a single woman than "slim pickin's." I arrived at the theater before Franklin and had time to pick up the tickets. When I went back outside to wait in front of the theater, I saw him walking across 13th Street. I was pleasantly surprised. He had on a navy-blue cashmere coat, black suit with a red tie, and black shoes. Actually he looked rather distinguished. I thought to myself, "This might not be too bad after all." For the most part, we enjoyed the play even though there was a brief point when he was disrespectful when he used the "MF" word during a conversation. Other than that, it felt good to be out on a date in the city. It had been a long time. After we left the play, he suggested we have dinner at his favorite Chinese restaurant in Chinatown. He loved this particular restaurant's Peking duck. I had eaten duck before, but I am not partial to it because of its high fat content. However, that night, dinner was delicious. We had an enjoyable meal topped off with my favorite wine, a red Sauvignon, and his usual Courvoisier. After dinner, he drove me to my car and I drove home, where we met briefly before he headed back to Palmer Park, Maryland.

CHAPTER 28
HUSBAND NUMBER SIX

The lion's den — vulnerable to a snarling wild carnivorous beast waiting to kill because that's his nature.

Abused women: living with the enemy — the beatings, the bruises, the broken bones, the black eyes, the covering of faces, protecting breasts, shielding stomachs, covering ears, closing eyes, loose bowels, stressed bladders, and silent prayers. But the enemy always finds a vulnerable open spot — with his fist, his feet, a gun or his tongue. He changes his physical appearance, becoming a roaring lion — dilated pupils, salivating, fist positioned to attack at the least provocation, bulging veins, screaming, rage — she's trapped in a closed environment waiting to be beaten or killed.

—Nesa Chappelle, Ph.D.

On Valentine's Day 2004, Franklin sent roses to my office. I was surprised and delighted. Since my father's death, I could not remember the last time I received anything for Valentine's Day. That same night, Brenda; her husband, Junie; Franklin and I went out to dinner. I was happy to spend a special evening with the three of them. After dinner and cocktails, Brenda and Junie went home and Franklin and I went to my house. Of course, he had quite a few drinks, and when we arrived at my house, he immediately fell asleep on the sofa while I retired to my bedroom upstairs. I heard him stirring early the next morning, a Saturday. I came downstairs and we talked briefly before he left to return to Palmer Park. I immediately went back to bed, content with the way things were.

After Valentine's Day, Franklin began to come around every day, but never stayed late into the night. I believe this was when my denial kicked in. Because Franklin was giving me constant attention, I began to let my guard down. I cannot say that he knew the right things to say and do, because he did not. His mouth was foul, especially when he was drinking.

It can be disastrous when a woman is lonely, especially if she believes that a man is what makes her life complete. The danger is when a relationship is "unhealthy" and I was in an unhealthy relationship — no, I was in a toxic relationship, one that slowly and steadfastly destroys anything that is good. Franklin began to talk all the time about changing his life and I continued to encourage him to get his own place. He didn't want that. I knew that he wanted to live with me! I told him that the next man I lived with would be my husband. That's how the subject of marriage came about.

It is important to know the dynamics of alcoholics and addicts to understand the gist of what I am sharing with you. When Franklin was not drinking, he was kind and considerate. Nonetheless, people like Franklin, who are plagued with alcohol addiction, are weak, making it easy for evil spirits to take over their minds, bodies, and souls. If you don't believe in evil spirits or demons, I am here to tell you that they absolutely do exist. I did not know or understand this phenomenon at the time — it's something that I learned much later, and it is something that is vitally important to share with my readers, especially women

When I bought the shell of a house on Capitol Hill seven years earlier, I did so with the intention of renovating and then flipping it to buy my dream home that was to be a luxurious condo in downtown DC. The housing boom was at its peak when Franklin crawled back into my life. It was a time when I was preparing to take the leap and sell my beautifully renovated Capitol Hill rowhouse. However, I was in no hurry to sell, because the condo I had my eye on was still under construction. Franklin became a steady part of my life and I finally and reluctantly let him move in. I made up my mind that I would not live with another man who was not my husband and Franklin knew this. So, when he moved in with me, we began to make plans to marry. Now that he had moved into my space and became comfortable, his abuse of alcohol was undeniably a serious problem, but I convinced myself that we could work through his drinking. All he needed was my love and support. I also noticed that he was uncomfortable around my friends, who were successful and well-educated. Whenever he was in their presence, I sensed he was intimidated and felt out of place.

In hindsight, this was the mistake I continued to make — trying to fix the wrong man instead of waiting for the God-sent man. I knew in my heart that it was wrong to marry him. It was like living in a "Twilight Zone."

I continued studying for the doctorate, working, and planning a wedding. I knew this would be my last marriage and I wanted it to be super-special. Believe it or not, as time went on, I was ecstatic that I was getting married again. I talked myself into believing that we were closing the circle because we were together very briefly in the past and now we came full-circle and would be together again permanently.

I put the Capitol Hill house up for sale. Franklin was adamant that he did not want to live in a condo — he stressed that he did not want to live around a lot of people. Because I believed in compromise, his scheme sounded plausible at the time and I agreed on a single-family home. I called my lifelong friend, Egypt C.J. Dawson, who sold me the Capitol Hill home, and had her put the house on the market. I was worried that the house would not sell quickly because it was customized specifically for my lifestyle as a single person. During renovation of the house, I put in central air conditioning, a fireplace, and a downstairs bathroom tiled in a soft gray. Spanish ceramic tile covered the foyer leading into the house, while the floors were an exotic white wood. A pantry with a chest freezer was off the kitchen, which led outside onto a cement patio that I had built a few years back. In the spring and summer, I enjoyed meals and libations on the patio. The entire upstairs of the house was a suite with a huge bedroom, ample closets, a separate room for the toilet, and a Jacuzzi and shower in the back of the house. It was a dream home for a single person. Egypt thought the house would take longer to sell than usual because it had only one bedroom. I had recently started the renovation on the basement, but, after deciding to sell, left it unfinished.

I excitedly made preparations for the wedding that was three months away: choosing the invitations, the cake, the place where we would marry, the honeymoon, the outfits, and the person who would perform the ceremony— everything. Franklin referred to the wedding as a "circus" and did not try to comprehend why I refused to go to a justice of the peace. I adamantly told him I wanted to be married by an ordained pastor. I wanted a "holy" marriage and that was the biggest joke I ever played on myself.

The wedding arrangements were made and I paid for everything. He did put my wedding ring on his charge account, but I ended up paying for it out of the household money. At first, he told me he would not wear a wedding ring. I said, "Fine, we won't get married." He hurriedly agreed to wear a wedding ring once he realized that there were some things that I refused to compromise on. I had his band made with clustered diamonds in the middle on a sculptured band. He did not offer to put one dime toward the wedding, but he was busy getting his homeys together to participate in the wedding — his scheme was working!

The garden wedding was held at a friend's house in Upper Marlboro, Maryland. It was a beautiful day in early May — a bit on the cool side but absolutely gorgeous. I wore a beautiful lime-green floor-length gown with a matching headband. My makeup was impeccable. Franklin wore a beige suit with a multi-colored tie. My maid of honor and three bridesmaids wore beige dresses, while the men wore beige suits. My son, Richard, casually dressed in dark slacks and a white shirt, gave me away. The wedding was absolutely beautiful and expertly catered. We said our vows in a beautiful white gazebo with approximately sixty guests in attendance. I suppose most were there to witness the "circus," but I was so happy and I believed Franklin was happy. His "con" worked — so far.

There were many signs along the way that my relationship with him was absolutely wrong. Shortly before the ceremony, he panicked when he realized that he left his tie at the rowhouse. He ran out with his male entourage in tow to find a tie to wear with his suit. He didn't think to borrow a tie from one of the men already at the house. The wedding was delayed by one hour and his friends were nervous that he might not return. As we were waiting for Franklin to return for the ceremony, I peeked out of the bedroom window and saw men in beige suits on cell phones trying to contact him to determine if he had developed cold feet and if I was being stood up. I sat on the bed not the least bit worried — I knew he would be back. Finally, along with his entourage, he drove up to the front of the house. He jumped out of the car and ran upstairs to put on his tie.

To keep the guests from being bored and annoyed, the woman hired to sing at the wedding provided music while he was chasing his tie. The guests were happy and satisfied with the food and the music. The time came for the wedding party to get in position when my maid of honor noticed ghetto Franklin had on his black nylon ghetto skullcap. She reminded him that he was wearing it and he quickly removed it. He forgot he had it on and was in the process of stepping out of the door on his way to the gazebo in front of our guests to marry me. What a nightmare that would have been!

The wedding went smoothly, just as it had been rehearsed. I was so nervous I was shaking like a leaf on a tree on a windy day. Franklin looked deep into my eyes as he falsely said he would love, honor, and respect me. After taking our vows, we greeted our guests as husband and wife. Of course, we took time to pose for pictures and meet each other's friends and family. A few members of his family came from South Carolina to attend the wedding. The reception was frenzied with laughter, dancing, food, and happiness.

Our flight left Reagan National Airport on Monday morning after the wedding so that we would spend our honeymoon on Captiva Island in Florida. It pains me to write that he wore that ugly black ghetto skullcap on our honeymoon. I had decided not to make a big deal about it because that would only encourage him to stubbornly refuse to remove it. We arrived in Florida, rented a car, and drove to Captiva Island. After checking into the hotel, we found the lounge and had lunch. The island was breath-takingly beautiful. When I had attended a business meeting there a few years prior, I promised myself that if I ever married again, I wanted to honeymoon there. Long strips of beautiful golden sand and turquoise water lined the island. The weather was perfect — a warm sun to bathe a tired body and soul after quickly and stressfully preparing for a wedding. Franklin was true to his word; he was not a sociable person, preferring to stay in the room, drinking Courvoisier and looking at the ignorant tube. We did go out to eat, but when I suggested we ride around the island he was not interested. What a bore!

My honeymoon on Captiva Island would be a sign of times to come. The first thing that happened to me while on the honeymoon was that I began to bleed vaginally. I was petrified. I'd had a hysterectomy, but yet I was bleeding. Imagine bleeding on your honeymoon and you don't know why or how. Franklin immediately called a doctor that he knew at the hospital where he worked to tell him about my symptoms. By the time the doctor returned his call, the bleeding had subsided. He told Franklin to bring me in to see him as soon as we got back home. (When we arrived home, I went straight to see the doctor Franklin had contacted. A sonogram was done and nothing could be found as to why I experienced bleeding.) The second incident happened two nights before we left Captiva Island. I convinced Franklin to go out on the beach and sit with me after dinner one evening. While sitting on Captiva's gorgeous beach, I was unknowingly eaten alive by "no see ums" — microscopic bugs that wreaked havoc on my legs.

The third incident occurred a day after we left the island. A hurricane developed and literally tore the island in half. The fourth incident occurred when we returned home. I found my son in the hospital after he had been in a terrible motorcycle accident while I was gone and was seriously injured. He had to be taken by helicopter to the hospital. Richard forbade anyone to tell me about the accident while I was in Florida because he wanted me to enjoy my honeymoon. I thought I would lose my mind when I saw my baby, but was reassured that with time and physical therapy, he would recover. His rehabilitation was long, arduous, and frustrating for him.

Husband Number Six

When I was comfortable that Richard would recover, I left his bedside for a few moments to go to the emergency room to check on the "no see um" bites I received. Both legs were full of grossly open, hideous seeping sores. It was a horrible sight. The emergency room doctor explained to me that I was allergic to the urine from the bugs and gave me three prescriptions. Franklin had minimal "no see um" bites and no adverse reactions. The "no see ums" wanted no part of him. I spent the next few weeks helping Richard where I could and being a good wife.

CHAPTER 29

THE HONEYMOON IS OVER

Shortly after returning from our honeymoon, Franklin and I began to seek newly built homes in the Prince George's County area. In 2004, the housing market was booming and there were minimal lots available on which to build new homes. After becoming discouraged about the scarcity of lots, we found a builder who had a few lots left in a convenient area. The location was ideal — close to the Beltway and right off of Pennsylvania Avenue Extended. The builders promised us that we would be in our new home in six months, but it took more than a year. Thankfully, before finally finding the location for our new home, the house on Capitol Hill was sold. I was more than relieved. I was having anxiety attacks about the possibility of having two mortgages. As it turned out, there was absolutely no need to worry. Because the builder did not have our house ready by the time promised in the contract, two things could have happened: (1) The contract would become null and void; or (2) If the builder agreed, we could negotiate a new contract. If a new contract was negotiated, the price of the house could be increased. Luckily, we were offered the exact contract as previously negotiated. The builder did not start construction on the house until more than one year after signing the first contract.

After the DC home was sold, Franklin and I rented a small, two-bedroom apartment across the bridge in Shirlington, Virginia. I could not believe the rents people were paying for apartments. I was totally shocked. I was forced to put most of my furniture and clothes in storage because, of course, the apartment was hardly large enough to hold one-quarter of my belongings. We leased the apartment for six months, but I was doubtful that I could do one day over the term of the lease. Franklin was enamored with Virginia, but it was not my favorite place by any means. For some reason, he appreciated Virginia because it was a commonwealth state. Of course, there had to be a political reason to demonstrate his "intellect" when asked why we moved to Virginia.

We moved from the house into the apartment with the help of his nephews and friends. The move was more than traumatic. It was unbelievably disorganized. The moving catastrophe was the first time I witnessed how lazy and trifling Franklin really was. He did as little as possible. He was more of a nuisance than help to the movers to the point that they were extremely irritated with him. Here was a man who thought he was too intelligent for "manual labor" and believed that everyone else should do the backbreaking work, while he supervised and sipped Courvoisier. He was absolutely worthless. He always reminded me that he "don't do no mothafuckin' manual labor. Only ignorant niggas and slaves do that shit." I can't remember the many times during the move that my blood silently boiled.

We finally settled into the apartment, and I went about the business of making our temporary home as cozy as possible and planning the design of the home being built. Now that we were out of my home, and living as man and wife in an apartment leased by both of us, the real Franklin emerged. To provide a background, we agreed that, when we found a house, he would have to come up with the required deposit. I was not going to be the only one to invest in the house. After all, his name would be on the mortgage as well as mine. Franklin borrowed $5,000 from his credit union for the initial deposit on the house. My resources, including the proceeds from the sale of my Capitol Hill home, enabled me to make more than the required down payment so that the monthly mortgage payments would be manageable. To be debt-free at settlement, I also paid off the $5,000 loan that Franklin borrowed from his credit union for the initial deposit.

The time came to select options for our new home. I was like a child in a candy store, excited about the many options available for the new house. I have a unique eye for color that is different and bold. I spent an exorbitant amount of time visiting model homes, reading interior design books, attending home expos, and paying attention to décor in hotels as I traveled extensively for business. Given my taste and interior design skill, I was not satisfied with the standard options. I opted to upgrade everything — two fireplaces (one in the family room and the other in the upstairs master bedroom); skylights installed in the sunroom and the upstairs master bathroom.

A few weeks after the options were selected, the builder called to advise me that our options totaled $7,500 and that a check was needed in that amount. I excitedly called Franklin at work and told him what the builder required. He said, "We'll talk about it when I get home this evening." I was confused about what we needed to "talk about" because the money was due to the builder for the options that were chosen. Realizing that I was already overwhelmed with a demanding job that required extensive travel, studying for the Ph.D., building a new house, and adjusting to my marriage, I decided to send the $7,500 check to the builder. It would be one less pressure and one less thing on my mind. I had planned earlier that morning to have a cocktail after work with my friend who had been my maid of honor. Before joining her at the hotel for cocktails, I telephoned Franklin to let him know that I would not be straight home and told him that I had sent the check to the builder. I didn't give it a thought because I didn't think I had done anything wrong. He began to curse, scream, and shout at me on the phone like a madman. I was paralyzed. I could not believe that he was acting so stupid because, after all, it was my damn money that was building the house in the first place. I was so upset while having cocktails with my friend that she asked me to calm down and said that maybe Franklin had a hard day. I knew it was not that simple and I tried to enjoy the rest of our time together.

I arrived at the apartment and parked my car in the garage under the building, took the elevator to the second floor, walked a few feet to our apartment, put the key in, and opened the door. I walked in and said, "Hello." I looked at him, and in an instant knew he had been drinking, but that was nothing new. But there was something different about him that night. He immediately went nuts, screaming, "I ain't no white/black motherfucka. You use to them intellectual niggas who don't know nothin'. Bitch, I'm mothafuckin' Franklin Carter, bitch!" It was unbelievable. I could not believe he was talking to me like that. I retorted, "You will not talk to me like that." He said, "You a stupid bitch. You believe anything a white motherfucka tell you; you just gave the fuckin' money away. They tell your stupid ass anything." I attempted to explain to him that the money would be applied at closing. By this time, he was in my face yelling and screaming. It was the first time among many to come that I would actually see him physically transform into something that did not appear to be human. During his transformation, his eyes became red and bulged out of their sockets, his lips curled back like a wolf's, exposing his short, brown, dingy teeth to the point that I expected them to drop and grow sharp fangs like a vampire. That's when I knew without a doubt that I had married a demon. He was directly in my face screaming and cursing, calling me bitches and accusing me of dealing with "white/black motherfuckas" over and over again.

I realized there was no need to try to talk to him. I turned around to walk out of the door, when he grabbed me by my neck and pushed me into the closet. Instinctively, I balled my fist and hit him as hard as I could in his left eye. I hit him so hard that he fell backward over a maroon lounge chair. All that was visible after the punch were his legs, which were up in the air behind the chair. I was angry! I was mad! I challenged him to get up, come what may. He got up and backed away from me with his hand over his left eye, whining that I hurt his eye and surprised that not only did I knock the snot out of him, but I was ready for more. I was livid! I could not believe that I was in another abusive relationship.

As time went on, he became more smug in the fact that we were married. He would hurl insults at me and scream that "You're *my WIFE*"— how I hated it when he said that. Living with Franklin was intolerable. There were times when he was quiet, calm, and decent. He would pour himself a drink, go out on the balcony, and watch people — watch them for hours coming and going. Most of the time, he nursed his Courvoisier, looked at TV, sat on the balcony, and tormented me. He was unmistakably and unequivocally an alcoholic. We never had discussions; rather, there were challenges and debates. He didn't refer to a woman by her name but referred to her as "the bitch." We argued hundreds of times over that word and he would challenge me to get the dictionary to read Webster's definition of a bitch. This was to prove his point that a bitch was a "low-down woman." He always said nobody knew the dictionary like he did. I suspected that spending most of his life behind bars gave him plenty of time to study a dictionary and anything else he wanted to become proficient in.

I called our relationship "three up" because by his third drink, the demon was alive and well. The night before our first anniversary, he got drunk and out of nowhere began a fight. I asked him to please leave. He yelled that he didn't need me and he angrily stormed out of the apartment. My nerves were shot. There was absolutely no peace in my life. Misery and destruction were all he knew to bring to anything that was good. His language was so unbelievably foul that I could not hear him because of the downright dirty delivery. I was relieved that Franklin left, but peace never lasted long. He called later to tell me that he was going to kill himself. I asked him if there was anything I could do to help him make his transition. I wanted him to just go the hell away. Later, I learned that his behavior was characteristic of abusers, who look for sympathy and place blame on everyone but themselves. I tried to sleep, but was too emotionally devastated. Sleep would not come. Thoughts came to mind that his family would blame me if he did commit suicide, and I did not need that pressure. I remembered hearing about people reaching out to someone before actually committing suicide. As much as I wanted him gone, I couldn't handle it if I ignored him like I wanted to do and he did kill himself.

I angrily got out of bed and telephoned his sister, Carrie, in South Carolina and told her that he was threatening suicide. She told me to go back to bed, that he wasn't going to do anything. Damn, I said to myself — now what? I then telephoned his alcoholic cousin and partner, Ernest.

Arlene, Ernest's abused wife, answered the phone and told me that he was asleep. I told her what was happening and she said she would have Ernest call me in the morning. Either his family did not care whether he killed himself, or they had been through this with him before.

Something told me to check the garage where we parked our cars under the building. I threw a light coat over my nightgown, grabbed my keys, and took the elevator down to the garage. I saw the drunken demon asleep in his car with the windows closed, the motor running, and his head slumped on the steering wheel. I stood there looking disgustedly at him, wishing I could just let him die, hating him for turning my world upside down. I took the spare key to his car that I kept on my key ring, opened the door, and angrily shook him awake. I bitterly told him to get out of the car and go upstairs to the apartment. He was despicable. By the time I took my coat off, he was asleep on the sofa in a drunken stupor. It was 3:00 a.m. — happy first anniversary to me!

Later that morning, characteristic of abusers, he apologized and promised he would stop drinking. I rolled my eyes at him. I knew exactly what I was married to. I felt like I was stuck in cement, with my heart broken, dreams shattered, and hard-earned money tied up in a house being built. I certainly could not walk away from the contract without losing a lot of money. People may say that money is not everything and they are undeniably correct, but try starting over in late middle-age. I couldn't do it; wouldn't do it.

I was more than ashamed of myself for marrying a loser when I saw the signs as clear as day before I said "I do." I was unable to fathom how to get out of the mess I allowed myself to get into. Getting rid of Franklin would be next to impossible without putting my finances and resources at risk. I was more worried about a financial loss than a physical threat. I often reminded him that I came from the same streets as he did; the only difference is I took the high road. There are things you never forget when you survive the streets. He figured he had me and he could do whatever he wanted to me because I was *HIS WIFE*. He didn't take into consideration that I was the daughter of a real hustler and knew what to do when backed into a tight corner. My father taught me the skill of survival. I began to clandestinely plan to get rid of Franklin, to end the joke of a marriage.

CHAPTER 30

A New House, But Not a Home

N erves raw, my money tied up, and trying to get a Ph.D. was too much for any one person to bear. I tried to study for my doctoral comprehensive examinations, but nothing was going right for me. Even though Franklin would come in late from work to supposedly give me time to study, there was no peace or support in my life. He pretended to support me in my dream of obtaining a Ph.D., but his actions proved otherwise. The apartment was much too small to spread out my study material, not to mention the fact that my husband was a bona fide mental case. I was a messed-up abused woman trying to find a way out of no way. Believe me when I tell you that nobody can beat you up worse than yourself when you know you've screwed up — that's the worst butt-whipping you can have. I was kicking myself in my rear until it was black and blue. Still, I was trying to keep peace at home as best I could.

The day of my first comprehensive exam, I awoke early, showered, grabbed my notes, and headed out the door. Franklin had the nerve to wish me luck. I calmly drove to the university in plenty of time to go over my notes before the examination began. Realistically, I should not have taken the exam at that time because I was mentally, emotionally, and spiritually depleted. I was not even one hundred percent clear about the foundation of the field for the exam being undertaken. I was unhappy, ashamed, fearful, and uncertain as to what the future held for me. A few weeks later, I received a letter from the university on the results of the comprehensive examination. As I suspected, I failed it. I was numb even though I knew I did poorly on the exam. It was the first time I had ever failed an examination and I was devastated. What little confidence I had left evaporated. The letter informed me that I could take the examination once more but, if I failed the second time, I would be dismissed from the program and the university. What was happening to my life? Oh God, please don't let me fail — stand by me — I can't do this alone. I began to accept that fact that what was happening to me was a consequence of being disobedient to God because He warned me on many occasions not to marry Franklin. I would understand even more as time passed. The times when I felt I could not make it another day, His calm voice would whisper, *"Be still and know I am God — no weapon formed against you shall prosper."* I grew up in the church and have always believed in God, but somewhere along the way, my priorities got skewed. You don't really know Him until you are down and have nowhere else to look but up. There comes a time when God is the only one you can talk to; the only one who can lead you out of the wilderness; the only one who can shield you against Satan's warfare; the only one who slaps the hand raised to hurt you; the only one who sends angels to help you through situations when you least expect it; and ultimately, the only one who can cause Satan to retreat when his goal is to destroy you at whatever cost. *Be still and know I am God* – listening to that is how I survived.

We moved into the beautiful newly built house in July 2006. I was relieved to finally be in the house, but at the same time I was sad because I knew I had to get Franklin out of my life. He had to go before someone got hurt. The first night in the house, we slept on an air mattress because we had not yet retrieved the furniture out of storage. Franklin jumped up at every little noise and creak as the house was settling. I lay in my beautiful new home in awe — the only flaw was Franklin was there.

Living in the house with him revealed what I had come to know. He knew absolutely nothing about taking care of a house. What perturbed me most was that he didn't want to learn. He kept insisting that he "don't do no motherfuckin' manual labor." I mentioned to him one day that we needed to pay attention to the front yard because our home was on the main road and I wanted to have a nice "curb appearance." He replied, "I

A New House, But Not a Home

ain't into no mothafuckin' aesthetics — I ain't like you, trying to keep up with the motherfuckin' Joneses." He never ceased to amaze me. I told him that this was his home and he should want to make it look nice. I consciously made a decision to include him on plans about enhancing the house to avoid drama. Whenever I wanted to hire contractors to work on the house, he had problems with it. He wanted to bring in his ex-con buddies to do work. His philosophy was not to pay people. According to him, his friends would do it for beer and chicken, and that's what their work looked like — beer and chicken.

I bought a beautiful light post from a home exhibit show that I wanted placed in the front yard. One of his hoodlum friends, supposedly an electrician, was to do the installation. He came to the house a couple of times, but did not install the light post in the yard, telling us that he would be back. I waited for more than two months and the guy never came back to install the light. I later hired a licensed electrician to install it, and told Franklin that I did so. Because the electrician was not one of his irresponsible hoodlum friends, he showed his butt when he came home and the electrician was working in the basement examining the electrical panel. When the electrician came up from the basement, Franklin began his antics — using foul language and disrespecting me in front of him. "Come here, Nesa," he demanded. I calmly suggested we talk after the electrician left. He bellowed, "We are going to talk now." As usual, I ignored him. Then he said, "Don't make me get up and come over there." I simply looked at the lunatic. The electrician, who I could sense was uncomfortable, went out front to complete the installation.

I left the house and sat on the front steps to watch, as is my custom whenever contractors are providing a service. Franklin slithered out of the house through the garage with his glass of Courvoisier and ordered me to come to him. When I ignored him, he threatened me as to what would happen if he had to call me again. I sat there completely ignoring him. He was always challenging, controlling, disrespecting, or trying to intimidate me. He walked toward me and I stared directly into his eyes, which told him, "Don't even think about it," and he went back into the house. I apologized profusely to the electrician — embarrassed again.

Before he left, he urged me to get out of that situation. He told me I deserved much better than what I had. After the electrician left, I went inside the house where Franklin proceeded to give me the speech that I could recite from memory. His verbal attacks usually started with "I am motherfuckin' Franklin Carter" and I learned to back him off by asking "and who is he?" He could never answer that. I ignored his threats about "humps in the ground" and intimidation tactics such as, "Bitch, I'll cut your mothafuckin' throat and eat a sandwich while you bleed to death." I never displayed fear to him because I knew that if I did, it would be all over. At first, I didn't know what "humps in the ground" meant until I asked my gangsta brother, Toby. According to him, it referred to buried bodies.

Another night, he decided to wreak havoc on me again. This time, he placed a phone call supposedly putting a "hit" out on me. He wanted me to hear the conversation. I don't know who he was talking with, but it definitely sounded genuine to me. He has the uncanny ability to control those with weak minds. His thug friends do not have minds of their own and look up to idiots like Franklin to lead them. So, in my mind it was feasible that one of his cronies would carry out such an order. I was sick and tired of his childish, wicked games. I became hysterical and uncontrollable; then he apologized saying, "Girl, I'm just playing with you; you know I would never hurt you." That night I was tired, fed up, exhausted, and angry. I looked him straight in his eyes and said, "I'm going to get you."

On another night, while I was studying in bed preparing to take the second comprehensive exam, Franklin arrived home later than usual. Everette, his pitiful protégé nephew, was there. Everette was who he used to do everything in the house that he should have been doing himself. I cooked dinner as usual and because Franklin had not come in from work, I wrapped his plate and placed it in the refrigerator. I heard him enter the house, climb the stairs and come into the bedroom. Out of the blue, he started in on me again.

"Did you eat?"

"Yes," I replied.

"Who else ate?"

"Everette."

"Oh, you feed everybody except *your HUSBAND?*"

I knew this would be one of those nights, but I was not feeling it. I told him that I put his food in the refrigerator and all that he needed to do was to put it in the microwave. He raised hell. I don't know to this day what brought that tirade on, but I suspect he was out doing something he had no business doing — guilt. I tried to ignore him, and suddenly he snatched my textbook out of my hand. Before I knew it, I jumped up, and in my fury, tried to tear his eyes out. Everette heard the commotion and ran into the bedroom screaming for Franklin to leave, while pulling me off of him. I was hysterical, crying; I was steadily trying to get to Franklin, but Everette held onto me tightly, not giving me an inch to tear his eyes out. He had to die. He just had to die that night. Everette screamed at Franklin to leave the house, but he refused, saying, "I just need to talk to my wife." Everette was furious with Franklin and kept screaming at him to leave, but Franklin would not. That night I knew it had to end and soon. I feverishly prayed to God to get that demon away from me. *"Be still and know I am God"* were the constant words that I heard.

One summer afternoon, Franklin took his keys, including the keys to my Jaguar, outside with him while he smoked a cigarette. After a short time, he came into the house and told me that he lost the keys to the Jaguar. We looked everywhere in the yard but never found the keys. I told him to change the locks to the house and to my Jaguar. He changed the locks to the house, but refused to get my Jaguar re-keyed. I argued with him that someone might steal my car. "I know mothafuckin' criminal minds; ain't nobody gon' fuck with the Jag." I stayed on him about re-keying my car, but he steadfastly refused, saying that we did not have the money. That was ludicrous! Of course, he could have the car re-keyed using my money, but because he knew it was something I wanted, he refused. I could have taken care of it myself, but I was determined that I was not going to play "mama" to him and that this was one time he was going to be held accountable.

One morning as I was sleeping, I heard the doorbell. I sleepily pushed the intercom and asked who was there. "Prince George's County police, ma'am." I looked out of the peephole to be certain that it was, in fact, a police officer, and I opened the door. He greeted me: "Good morning, ma'am. Do you own a 2003 Jaguar?"

"Yes," I replied.

"Do you know where it is?"

"It's in the driveway." I replied.

"No ma'am; it's been stolen and totaled."

I was in a state of shock. He told me where the car was taken. Someone stole the car with the lost or stolen keys and wrapped it around a tree in Upper Marlboro, Maryland. I was livid, and immediately called Franklin — all he ever did for me was cause me heartache and cost me money. He came home immediately and took me to see my car. When I saw the car that I waited thirty years to buy totaled, I just cried. Franklin had fake tears in his eyes, saying, I'll buy you another Jag. The truth is he couldn't buy himself a pair of shoes, but he was going to buy me another Jag.

I was devastated. I certainly could not afford to buy another Jaguar, even with the insurance money I got as a result of the theft. The police treated the crime as just another stolen vehicle, but I would not let it rest. I stayed in touch with the investigating officer and put as much pressure on her as I could. After asking around in the neighborhood, a neighbor told Franklin that a fifteen-year-old neighborhood hoodlum found the keys and decided to impress young girls at his school by driving my car. He was arrested, but because he was a juvenile, nothing happened to him at all. His mother had to pay $300 and she did so by sending a check for $30 through the court once a month until paid. Justice! That's another book.

CHAPTER 31
THE EXIT STRATEGY

I was attending a conference in Philadelphia in the summer of 2006 and was scheduled to give an important speech on Thursday. On Wednesday evening, I was comfortably resting in my hotel room preparing for my speech. Franklin telephoned me at the hotel, intoxicated as usual. He began to whine like a spoiled brat, complaining that I was not there with him. I replied that he was well aware of my professional obligations before we got married. Then, out of nowhere, he began to scream through the telephone demanding that I tell him how many "dicks" were waiting outside my room for me. He ranted and raved like a lunatic for about five minutes before I slammed the phone down. My pulse was racing. I was shaking. I didn't know what to do. I couldn't think. I was upset to the point that I became nauseated and physically ill. I turned my cell phone off so that he could not reach me. I was not about to indulge him in his nonsense, not that night. I knew he would call the hotel directly so I called the hotel operator and requested that a hold be placed on all calls to my room.

I tried to concentrate on my speech again, but my mind was in a fog. I was thankful that I traveled on business often because it provided down time from my dysfunctional life and psychopath husband. I called a co-worker, a much older woman also attending the conference and my office confidante. She came to my room immediately. She was married to a psychiatrist and understood the hell I was going through with Franklin. I confided in her what had just transpired. She looked at me with compassion and concern and said what she had always said to me: Get out, get away from him before he hurts you. She always told me, "He is jealous of your success and cannot handle the fact that he is not on your level." She pleaded, "Get out." She sat with me for a while and suggested I get some sleep because I needed to be prepared for my speech the following day. As she was leaving my room, she turned around and said to me again, "Get out. Leave him."

I awoke early on Thursday and prayed to God to speak through me to deliver a good speech. I prayed for Him to keep me safe and asked for His grace and mercy. I prayed for strength, courage, and patience — believing that I would be delivered. With shaking hands, I nervously applied my make-up, dressed in a beautiful white business pantsuit complemented by white-and-black heels. I took a deep breath, held my head high, and entered the meeting room with a fake smile of confidence. As I requested in prayer, the Creator led me through the speech, which I delivered with confidence, not forgetting a single important point. I performed superbly, but it was, however, only a performance. After the speech, I attended another meeting, had dinner with co-workers, and retired to my room to prepare to leave for Maryland the following afternoon.

On Friday morning, while in a taxi on my way to the train station, I knew that I could not go back to that hellhole called home. I boarded the luxurious southbound Acela train headed for Union Station in DC. The closer the train got to DC, the more traumatized I became. I decided to get off the train in Baltimore. I was not ready to go home. I was a wreck. I telephoned my attorney from Baltimore and, in desperation told him that I needed to see him first thing the next morning. He asked me to be at his office by 10 a.m. I then telephoned two of my friends, Angie and Sherry, and asked them to meet me for dinner that evening. I briefly explained to them what happened, and that I had to find a way to get away from Franklin. I was confused about how to get out of the marriage without causing myself irreparable financial ruin. Angie and I agreed where we would meet in downtown DC. She assured me that she would be there to pick me up. I called her when I arrived at Union Station, cautiously checking to make sure that Franklin was nowhere around searching for me. I was beyond paranoia. I quickly boarded the Red line Metro train, making my way downtown to where Angie and I were to meet. She was waiting for me when I reached 18th and K Streets NW. She quickly put my bag in her Mercedes and I slid in. We were to meet Sherry at a favorite Latin restaurant in DC's Adams Morgan community. We arrived at the restaurant and were seated, and I talked to Angie about how disappointed I was with myself for being in this mess. I asked myself what was I thinking about to fall into this trap with a man I knew was wrong for me. She tried to console me, reminding me that everyone makes mistakes.

During our conversation, Sherry arrived. We ate dinner and discussed my next move. Angie asked me to stay at her house in Aspen Hill, Maryland, that night, but I chose to stay with Sherry because she lived in upper Northwest DC, and it was easier for me to get to my attorney's office by subway by ten the next morning. I felt like a bag lady. No home I wanted to go to, no peace, just confusion and misery while traveling with a small rolling carry-on bag. When Sherry and I arrived at her house, I took a hot shower, put my nightgown on, and fell into bed. I was more than exhausted.

The next morning, Sherry had to take her Mercedes to the shop, so she drove me to the nearest subway station. I arrived at my attorney's office a little before ten. The receptionist asked me to have a seat, and said that Don, my attorney, would be out in a moment. He met me in the reception area and escorted me to his office. He looked at me and asked if I was all right. I told him I was just plain tired and fed up. He offered me a cup of coffee, but I refused, not having an appetite at all that morning. He asked me what was going on and I told him everything as clients are expected to do. We talked about Franklin's verbal and emotional abuse and control tactics, and he advised me about my divorce options. He strongly recommended that I leave the house and seek a protection order. One thing was for sure, I was getting a divorce at whatever cost.

We talked about property settlement, possible difficulties with Franklin, and his fee, which was startling. Some of what he told me did lift my spirits. He advised me to try to wait to file for divorce until October 2006 because at that time, Maryland's community-property law would change to an equitable-distribution law. This change would be in my favor since I am the one who put all the money into the house and was able to prove it. We talked for close to an hour and I left his office with a plan. Somehow, I would find the will to wait a couple of months until October 2006 to file for divorce — that's all I knew. I didn't know how or what the consequences would be but whatever they were, they could not be worse than things already were.

I stopped at the bank in the lobby of my attorney's office building to get cash. I then hopped on a train heading back downtown with my carry-on rolling bag in tow. Being a bag lady was a nuisance and a hassle. "How do the homeless survive?" I asked myself. I now clearly understood the term "bag lady" from a totally new perspective. The song by Erykah Badu, "Bag Lady," had a new meaning for me. Now, whenever I hear that song, I remember the "bag-in-tow."

I got off the train at the Farragut North station and walked to a restaurant close by to grab a light lunch. My stomach was queasy, but I knew I had to eat. I also had a plan and I meant to work the plan.

The hardest thing for me to do was to confide in my son, a police officer, about what had been happening to me, his mother, in my hellified marriage. I telephoned him at work and told him about my problems with Franklin. He calmly listened and asked me what I wanted to do. I tearfully told him I wanted him to come and get me. I told him I would hang around downtown until he got off duty. He got off early and came to the aid of his mother. The first thing he wanted to know was why I did not tell him what was going on earlier. I told him the truth — I was too ashamed. I told him that I wanted him to be proud of his mother and not think of me as stupid. He quietly said, "We all make mistakes, Ma. You should not feel like a failure. You made a mistake and now we have to fix it."

I went home with my son and rested. I needed more clothes and my wheels. Richard was not about to let me go to the house alone, nor was I going to go to the house alone — no way! The next day, Richard called Prince George's County police, and after identifying himself as a DC police officer, requested a "move assist." He drove me to my street where we parked "surveillance style" and waited for Prince George's

County's finest to arrive. During our wait, we watched Franklin leave the house and drive away. He's so intelligent and observant that he never saw us watching him. Within minutes he returned, more than likely after going to the corner store to buy cigarettes.

Shortly after Franklin returned to the house, a Prince George's police cruiser pulled up. My son explained the situation to the officer. They both walked over to me sitting in Richard's truck, and the officer explained that for now I was only to take essentials like clothing and medicine. I got out of the truck and the three of us walked up to the door and rang the doorbell. Franklin answered and was visibly shocked to see us standing on the porch. The police officer explained to him that I was there to pick up a few personal belongings. Franklin told the police officer that he could not come into the house. The officer stared at him. Franklin must have thought about his parole status, and decided not to make a scene. Richard and I had already entered the house and were on our way upstairs to get a few of my things. The officer came upstairs and again told me to get just what I needed for now and to get a protection order from the court. As I was leaving, Franklin said, "You don't have to leave, you built this house. I will leave." As I was walking away, I told him that when he left, I would return and not before.

I stayed with Richard about a week. I was worried about my house, the mail, bills, money, and his hoodlum friends destroying everything that I worked for. I thought about renting an apartment, but there was no way I could pay apartment rent and the mortgage. Franklin could not afford to pay even half of the mortgage, nor did he know how to be responsible. I made the difficult decision to return to the house with a strong plan. I knew in my heart that it would not be long before somehow this hell would be over. I just knew. I talked it over with my son, telling him that I had no plans to stay in the marriage. I needed time to figure out how and when, but in the meantime the mortgage and the bills still had to be paid.

I telephoned Franklin and told him that I was reluctantly returning home and what my conditions were. I returned home to a fully prepared dinner, which I did not touch. I couldn't stand him. He was to sleep in the guest bedroom and he agreed to do that. That lasted for two nights when he slithered into my bed, but I couldn't stand him being in my presence so he left me alone. As expected, it was not long before his antics started again, but because I had a plan, I had the resilience to tolerate his foolishness and go on with my life and totally ignore him. He continued harassing me about my former friend, Solomon, and calling me a bitch, and trying to make my life a living hell, but I had a plan. I did not know how it would all work out but somehow I knew that his time with me was short. It's called faith!

A few months later, in October, while drinking his treasured Courvoisier, Franklin started in on me again. His verbal assault had begun earlier that evening, an unprovoked assault, the last assault that I would endure from him, and it was an ugly encounter. Angry as usual — always angry about something. There was always some kind of drama involving or initiated by Franklin. I can't remember every detail, but I do remember that Franklin was in the kitchen dining area and I was standing at the edge of the family room. Out of nowhere, he began to rehash my former relationship with Solomon Hughes. Franklin shouted, clasping a bottle of beer in his hand, "He was nothing but a big, fat, stupid motherfucker!" And those were the kindest words about Solomon that came out of his mouth. Franklin continued degrading Solomon, belittling him, making fun of someone he did not know and had never even met. His ranting and raving was not unusual, and in fact, his attacks on me concerning Solomon had become a common occurrence.

You see, it wasn't Solomon my husband was directing his anger at, not really. It was me he was gunning for. Whenever he thought it was time for me to get my verbal, mental, and emotional whipping, time for him to show me who was in control, Franklin picked a fight. And he was never satisfied until he had let loose his rage on me like an unrelenting tidal wave. But on this particular day, I had enough. Regardless of what he said, I did not say a word. I grabbed the keys to my SUV, calmly left the family room, walked out of the door leading to the garage, and climbed into my GMC Envoy parked in the driveway. As I started the engine, I realized I hadn't bothered to get my glasses or my purse.

Franklin followed me out and positioned himself boldly at the front of my truck, his demeanor and demonic eyes daring me to so much as budge. I studied him through the front windshield. I was left with two choices: I could drive forward and run him over, or put the car in reverse and back up across my beautifully landscaped lawn and get the hell out of harm's way.

I decided that he was not worth my going to jail, so I put the pedal to the metal and backed across the lawn onto the roadway behind our beautiful home. Less than thirty minutes later, I knocked on the door of the house that I co-owned with my brother Toby. We talked at length about my crumbling, torturous, abusive relationship with my husband and the fact that I had to get away from him. As I was about to leave, he asked whether I was going to be safe at home, and I convinced him that I would be fine. The truth is, once I got home and Franklin laid eyes on me, I had no idea what was going to happen, but I also knew I did not want to involve Toby in my mess because he is known for his violent temper. I definitely did not want to be responsible for what might happen to him because of my situation. I was emotionally broken to the point that I did not have the strength to continue down this chaotic road. I was unbelievably tired.

When I got home, my husband's car was not in the driveway. "Thank you, Jesus," I whispered. I went into the house, let the dog upstairs from the basement, and climbed into my comfortable bed, savoring every temporary peaceful moment away from Franklin Carter. No cursing, yelling, screaming, threats, tug of war; no keeping me awake all night with his exhausting, sick mind games. Not this night. Blessed with relief, I fell into a tranquil sleep. Then the phone rang, startling me awake on the first ring. I looked at the clock; it was almost 2 a.m. I answered on the third ring.

"Hello," I whispered into the receiver.

"Nesa?"

"Yes," I whispered in a calm voice, all the while feeling my body quiver, with good reason. It was Slye, Franklin's criminal buddy, a middle-aged, gun-toting stick-up boy.

"I just saw Franklin being arrested," Slye said, with nervous excitement and sounding ill at ease. "The police had him handcuffed and he was sitting on the side of the curb in Suitland, Maryland. There was a bottle of beer on the roof of his car."

"Oh really," I said, unconcerned. The beer bottle surely wasn't any surprise to me. And it shouldn't have been to Slye. "Where did this happen?" I asked.

"On Silver Hill Road and Brooks Drive," Slye replied. "Take down my phone number," he said, ignoring my lack of interest or concern. "Let me know when you hear from him."

"Okay," I said, not once making note of his phone number. I hadn't heard a word from Franklin since I left the house early that evening. I didn't care where he was as long as he was not near me. I was relieved to know he would not come home that night, and went back to sleep — a restful sleep. Not more than an hour later, the phone rang again. I figured it was Slye, so I answered on the second ring. "Hello," I said, less than welcoming.

"Have you heard anything yet?" Slye asked, more anxious.

"No!" I snapped. "Franklin knows he's on parole. They're giving people who violate parole at least thirty-six months of jail time. They're not playing with these fools now."

"Naw," Slye said, his voice sounding confident. "He ain't go'n git nothing like that. Look, as soon as you hear from him, please call me."

I hung up the phone and tried to go back to sleep. Sleep was all I wanted. I sure didn't want to think about Franklin Carter. But this time I couldn't get back to sleep. I was growing restless and I couldn't stop myself from wondering what was going on this time. How was this nightmare going to undoubtedly affect me, and what was left of my life? Then the phone rang a third time. It was Slye.

"Still ain't heard nothing from him?" he asked.

"No!" I snapped again.

"Call me as soon as you hear from him! I don't care what time it is, give him my number and have him call me! I'm worried about him!"

"Yeah," I said, and hung up the phone. I had neither the energy nor desire to worry about the man who called himself my husband. I had done my best to be a good wife to a man who did not respect or appreciate me or anyone else, for that matter. He didn't want a wife. He wanted a mother who would take care of him and cater to his every sick whim. He wanted an object on which to unleash his rage at will. He wanted a piece of property that he could control like a robot. Though, interestingly, and thankfully, sex was not important to him at all. What a blessing!

After the constant interruptions, I finally managed to get four hours of sleep. I woke up exhausted and had to be in the office first thing for a meeting. I walked the dog, showered, and dressed, and began my commute to the office. Twenty-five minutes later, I was entering Washington, DC, when my cell phone rang. I glanced at the caller ID display and shuddered. It was Franklin.

"Hello," I snapped. I felt sick — like my worst nightmare was back. I just wanted him to go away and leave me alone, drop out of my life. I prayed to God to release me from that demon. I knew God understood that I was at my breaking point.

"Hey," Franklin said, in his deep, Barry White baritone voice. "I didn't come home last night 'cause I got locked up."

"For what?" I asked. "For having beer in the car?"

"No, it's more than that," he said, nonchalantly.

"What else?" I asked nervously, needing, but not wanting, to know.

"A gun charge," he said. "They found a gun in the car."

"How stupid can you be?" I screamed. "You know you're on parole! And just where did you get a gun?" Before he could respond, a chill went through my body. Had Franklin taken the antique gun, one of the only two heirlooms left to me by my deceased father? He knew how much I cherished it.

"It's your fault!" Franklin said, pointing the finger of blame at me just like he always did for everything that went wrong in his life. "You're always pressing me about money and shit! I was going to try to get some quick money for us, so you shut the fuck up!"

"Don't you dare blame me for your doing something so stupid," I yelled.

"Look, I'm walking down Pennsylvania Avenue because my car is impounded," Franklin said. "I need you to come and get me."

"Franklin, I'm on my way to work. I'm not coming to get you."

"I'm *your HUSBAND!* You're not coming to get your *husband*?"

"No!" I said, emphatically. I shut off my cell phone and went to work in a daze. At the office, I pretended nothing happened. None of my co-workers suspected a thing, even though I was numb as a result of Franklin's stupidity and the mere thought of lawyers, more chaos, and the possible loss of his job, which would add more financial burden on me. I mechanically plowed through my paperwork, answered every business call, and responded to all e-mails.

At the end of the day, I drove home — a beautiful home on the outside, but pure hell on the inside. It had been the home I envisioned and prayed would be filled with love and joy. It never happened. Franklin saw to that. Whenever I walked into the house, a feeling of dread enveloped me. This night would be no different. The TV was on, which meant Franklin was home. I could hear him, feel him, smell him — but there would be no abuse this night. Tonight he would want to be civil. He would want to talk and talk. He would ask me if I wanted or needed anything. He would ask if I wanted something to eat. He would apologize for his actions, because that's what he did whenever he was in trouble. He needed me to accept his fabricated reason for being arrested. He needed to figure out whom he could cajole into taking the rap for him this time; pointing his finger of blame at anyone other than himself. It was his pattern, his mode of operation. It was time to play those mind games that he thought he was so good at — the ongoing manipulation and sick control tactics. He needed to put together a scheme to stay out of jail. Scheming is when he believed he was at the top of his game and there was something I knew and I knew for sure — it was always about Franklin Carter. As soon as he got what he wanted, he would start the abuse all over and with a vengeance, pushing the envelope a little farther each time. He had mentally, emotionally, verbally, and physically worn me out with his yelling and screaming, his warped intellect, his illogical reasoning, his attempts to coerce and threaten me into submission.

It was not long before his homeys came by to scheme and lie to help him stay out of jail. His nephew protégé, Everette, agreed to lie for

Franklin as always and say that the gun was his, even though he was on probation himself. It's amazing how fools can encourage weaklings to do the wrong thing and believe they are entitled to use people to their benefit.

Franklin believed he had it all figured out. He took out a loan from a finance company to pay for an attorney to represent him on the charges. He knew I would not provide a dime toward his legal fees and he also knew I had nothing but disdain for him. Even though he did not follow procedures regarding the conditions of his parole by notifying his parole officer of his arrest, it was not long before she found out about it. I found it interesting that the officers who arrested him did not run a background check; otherwise, he never would have been released in the first place.

Franklin's actions were a definite violation of the conditions of his parole. His court date for the gun charge in Prince George's Circuit Court was set for late December 2006. By this time, according to Franklin, his attorney told him to hide until the court date. Dennis Winston, Franklin's attorney, had the idea that if he could have the case dismissed in Prince George's County, it was more than probable that the Parole Commission would dismiss the case as well. Following his attorney's advice, Franklin went into hiding. A U.S. marshal telephoned me at home on several occasions, asking if I knew where Franklin was. I told him I had no idea where Franklin was staying and neither did I care. I hoped he would find him, put him away, and throw away the key.

There were times when, like a sneaky fox, he would creep back to the house late at night, entering through the basement. The first thing he would do was pour himself a drink and sit down, which infuriated me — acting as if he owned the world, stupidly believing he could control me on the run. There was one instance when, like a thief in the night, he came in through the basement and took my hand, trying to head upstairs. I snatched my hand away and faking concern for him, told him how dangerous it was for him to be at the house because a search was taking place to find him. I told him how he was putting me in danger of going to jail for aiding and abetting a criminal. He said, "You're my wife. They can't do nothin' to you."

I was sick and tired of him playing me for stupid. He must have gotten the message because he hurriedly left. When he called again, I let him know that if he came to the house again, he would be arrested. He asked, "What ya mean by that?" I told him the marshals had the house under surveillance, which was not true. He stayed away from me from that point on — glorious peace on one hand and terror on the other. When he left, he took my SUV and left his car with me. He was paranoid that the marshals would be looking for his car. I didn't care, I just needed him to go away. After leaving, he continually badgered me about "being there for *your husband*." I wanted to be there all right, hoping he would never see the light of day again. He would hide from the marshals for two weeks before his court date.

I did not sleep well the night before he was to appear in court in December. I got up early and prepared to meet him at the courthouse at eight o'clock. He telephoned me that morning and told me to meet him in the courthouse cafeteria. I arrived promptly at court at eight o'clock and as I was parking his car on the courthouse lot, he pulled up beside me in my SUV. He had a fresh haircut and was wearing the expensive dark suit that I had bought him two years earlier. The suit always brought him compliments. He looked like Professor Carter that day instead of the evil man he really was.

We walked to the courthouse where he was to meet his attorney in the court's cafeteria. It was not long before Ernest joined him in the court cafeteria. He was the other alcoholic cousin who referred Franklin to Attorney Winston in the first place. As we were waiting in the cafeteria, Franklin did as I requested earlier: He had Ernest, who was a realtor, prepare a power of attorney for me to sign to take care of his business in case he was held in custody. I signed the POA and placed it in my bag for safekeeping. I was sure it would come in handy.

Attorney Winston arrived and he and Franklin moved away from me and Ernest to talk alone. When it was time to go upstairs to the courtroom, Franklin grabbed my hand, and I quickly snatched it away. I did not want to be near him, much less have him touch me. When we entered the courtroom, Franklin and I sat down in the back while waiting for his case to be called. I noticed two white expressionless males positioned against the left wall watching Franklin. I knew they were marshals.

Attorney Winston beckoned for Franklin to step outside of the courtroom to speak with him. Winston returned to the courtroom without Franklin. He had advised him to leave the court grounds and contact him later because a warrant had been issued for his arrest when he arrived at court. A few minutes later, despite Winston's instruction, Franklin returned to the courtroom with a strange look on his face. He sat on the bench next to me, not saying a word. I often remember the look on his face; it was one of defeat and surrender.

No more than two minutes after Franklin returned to the courtroom, the bailiff called him to the front of the courtroom, ordered him to place his hands behind his back (assume the position), handcuffed him, and led him into a back room where he would be transferred to DC Jail. "Thank you, Jesus," I silently cried. I left the courtroom and was standing in the hall when his attorney approached Ernest and me, apologizing for what just happened in the courtroom. I asked him why he would tell him to run when he knew that it would be worse for his client. He simply said that he believed, if he could get him in front of the judge before Franklin went before the Parole Commission, he could have gotten him off.

Needless to say, I was more than happy to see Franklin go away. I was exuberant! I have a strong philosophy, however, about justice and fairness. For an attorney who took an oath of truth and justice to tell a black man to run from agents of the United States of America is a set-up. There was no question that Franklin deserved to be in jail because he is definitely a menace to society; however, our Constitution guarantees justice for everyone and this is one instance where justice was forfeited by an arrogant white lawyer who acted like he was above the law. I am not referring to justice necessarily for Franklin, but for minority and poor citizens in general. Franklin deserved to go to jail, and Winston should have been disbarred.

CHAPTER 32
FRANKLIN RETURNS TO HIS ROOTS

Franklin was now in DC Jail awaiting his appearance before the Parole Commission to determine his destiny. He telephoned me several times, but I refused to answer most of his calls. I was not and never would be in the mood again for his mind games. When we did talk, he said I was the reason for his being in jail. From the beginning of our re-acquaintance, I repeatedly made it clear to him that if he went back to jail I would not visit him. I told him on numerous occasions that I would not pay for collect telephone calls from prison, nor would I send money for his jail account or "commissary" privileges, as I learned was the correct jargon. For whatever reason related to jail, I was not sending funds to him. As usual, he took me for stupid — being "motherfuckin' Franklin Carter" meant that everything was to unequivocally go as he ordered. Wrong! I was more than relieved that he was no longer in my space. The mere thought of him returning to the house was enough to make me want to vomit. I would rather clean up my dog's vomit than clean up his.

One evening, a female attorney from DC Jail called to talk to me about Franklin's case. Franklin had done what he was expert at; he conned someone into believing that he was completely innocent. His gift of gab was paying off, and I knew exactly what had transpired. This articulate, seemingly highly intelligent black man with a velvety sexy voice and an above-average vocabulary had charmed her, and she didn't even know what was happening. I listened to her tell me that Franklin should not be in jail and that he was innocent and she was going to do everything she could to get him released within two days. She told me how important it was for me to be at the hearing to support him, so that the parole commissioners would see him as a responsible married man. I could not believe what I was hearing. But then, when I put everything into perspective, it was easy to figure out how she could be so gullible. He was good at his game, but not good enough.

After learning that Franklin would more than likely be released from jail within two days, I knew what I had to do. There was no way I could allow him back into my life or my space. It was just not an option. After having a conversation with the DC Jail attorney, the following morning I drove up to the Prince George's Circuit Court to request a protection order against Franklin. I was visibly a jumble of nerves, fighting panic attacks and trying to brace myself against the assaults I knew would come from Franklin and his enabling family. The clerk at the court asked me if I was all right. I answered yes. I told her that I wanted to take out a protection order against my husband. She gave me the forms to complete and explained the procedure. I sat down, hands shaking, to fill out the form. When I completed the form, I was to return it to the clerk. I silently and tearfully asked myself, "How did I get here?" On the form, I explained the verbal, mental, and emotional abuse, as well as the murderous threats posed by Franklin. To get straight to the point, I feared for my life.

I returned the form to the clerk, who asked me to sit in the waiting area, and I would be called in to talk to the judge. I was pained and petrified. I understood that requesting the protection order was necessary, but I worried about its consequences.

When I was ushered in to appear before the judge, he was busy reading the legal complaint. He asked me a few questions. There was one question I will never forget as long as I live. He wanted to know why I stayed in the marriage. In other words, what took me so long to leave? I replied that at first I was trying to make my marriage work, but it got to the point where it became impossible to live with my husband. He looked at me like I was absolutely insane. Obviously, that did not make sense to him.

When an order is issued, both parties are required to appear before the judge within seven days for a decision. Because Franklin was already in jail, the judge was unsure whether he would be able to appear in court within the prescribed time. He pondered for what seemed like an eternity. Finally, he decided to grant the protection order. He sensed that I was in trouble and needed the court's help, or perhaps he thought about the women who were maimed or murdered when judges refuse to grant a protection order.

Whatever it was, I was relieved and terrified at the same time. I drove home with mixed feelings. Franklin's mother was very ill and I worried about her dying before she saw her son again. If he was not released, I worried that his family would blame me for his being back in jail. On the other hand, I was confident that I did what I had to do to safeguard my life and my sanity. I did not know what Franklin might do because he always bragged about humps in the ground that he was responsible for.

Later that evening, I called Franklin's attorney and advised him that I had taken out a protection order. He stated, "Well, I will just have to send someone to pick up his clothes." At least with a protection order, he would be in violation of his parole if he attempted to contact me.

Two days later, Franklin appeared before the Parole Commission for an initial hearing. At first, the commissioners were prepared to release him until his hearing date, which would have been scheduled within a few weeks. However, when the commissioners pulled up his information on the computer, the protection order appeared. As a result of the order, and because of the gun charge, he was held pending a hearing. After he was denied release, he immediately blamed me for lying, causing him to not be released. He was more than infuriated — he was good and crazy!

As expected, his family began to call me to demand that I drop the protection order because their mother was dying and he needed to be home. "He should have thought about that before violating his parole," is what I said to them. His sister, Jocelyn, at sixty years old, is married to an old crack head who drives her crazy — yet she is calling and screaming at me, calling me a witch, and threatening me as to what "I had better do."

Before taking out a protection order against Franklin, I had a decent relationship with Regina, his oldest sister. The most important thing to her was that I stay married to her brother to keep the pressure off of her, the soon-to-be matriarch of the family. What she feared most about her brother was his going back to jail. His family enabled his foolishness for years, not realizing that it was doing him more harm than good.

Franklin was sentenced to 18 months in a federal penitentiary in North Carolina. He was charged with three offenses: felony possession of a handgun, handgun in vehicle, and alcoholic beverages in a vehicle on public property. I wish I could report that I was relieved, but my hell had no end. I continued to refuse his telephone calls and did not open his letters. When a letter from him arrived, my stomach dropped to my feet. I was terrified to go to my mailbox. I felt like I was living in a twilight zone; that none of this could be real — it just couldn't be.

I filed for divorce in January 2007. He was served with divorce papers while still in DC Jail, before being transferred to North Carolina. His family was outraged with me because they believed every lie he told them, even though they knew he was a liar and a criminal. It was more than obvious that he spent his time in prison scheming and planning ways to destroy me. During his incarceration, there was no doubt in my mind that he was a serious mental case.

While Franklin and I were married, at his request, I co-signed for an increase on his line of credit from $5,000 to $10,000 at his credit union. He was deranged to the point that he alleged that I, along with the credit union manager, conspired to fraudulently obtain a loan in his name without his knowledge. He also alleged that he had not signed a loan document for the $10,000, nor had he asked for an increase. When the credit union advised me of this matter, I searched the files at home and found the application with his signature. During all of this, Franklin used his sister Regina to do his dirty work. At one point, I actually felt sorry for her. By now, I knew Franklin well enough to know that he was desperate to hurt me and capable of anything.

On top of all the chaos I was already experiencing, I received a letter advising me that I failed my doctoral comprehensive examination a second time. I was informed that not only was I out of the Ph.D. program; I was forever out of all programs at the university. At this point, I just did not care anymore. There was too much going on; I could not handle another thing.

In December 2006, when Franklin was in DC Jail, his mother was in a rehabilitation center in DC, which was in the same building that housed the hospice center where my mother died. I believe the disappointment she felt regarding Franklin's return to prison was more than she could bear. I know she was tired and ready to die. Her children didn't want to be bothered with her and I believe that's why she wanted to go back home to South Carolina. Her grandson, Everette, and later her son, Michael, left Maryland and went to South Carolina to take care of her in her last days.

In August 2007, Franklin's mother passed away in her beloved South Carolina. She had been sick for years with congenital heart problems. She loved Franklin like only a mother can love a psychopathic wayward child. No matter what he did, or how many times he went to jail, she was there for him. Though he disrespected her, hurt her, and placed her in financial hardship with ongoing legal bills and prison expenses, she remained by his side. She loved her family, especially Franklin's daughter. Once, while visiting her family in Maryland, Franklin's mother became ill and had to be hospitalized. Upon her release from the hospital, she stayed with me and Franklin to recuperate. I took care of her as best I could with the huge responsibilities that I already had. Her daughters were not interested in sharing the burden of caring for their ailing mother. When it became too much for me to handle alone, I telephoned them to let them know that they had to help care for their mother. Carrie, the one daughter who lived right next door to her mother in South Carolina, did not want to provide care for her at all. After a conversation with Regina, she began to come to our house to feed her mother breakfast in the mornings and Jocelyn would come a few times during the week to prepare her dinner. None of them bothered to help us buy food. Regina often told me that Franklin wanted his mother to stay with us out of guilt for his being away from her so long because of his many incarcerations.

With Franklin's mother gone, Regina became the matriarch. The fact that Franklin was always blaming me for his screw-ups and his inability to see his mother before she died caused me great distress, but I knew better than most that he was his own worst enemy.

There was always something going on concerning Franklin. After his mother's death, I began to get e-mails threatening my life and condemning me for Franklin's predicament, promising "southern justice," whatever that was. I called the Prince George's County police and they immediately dispatched an officer to my home. We talked about what happened and he asked that I print out the e-mails so he could have them investigated. The police attempted to trace the e-mails, but because I copied them and moved them to another file, they could not be traced. If I had left it as it arrived, the perpetrator(s) could have been identified.

Regina was one of the individuals questioned by the police regarding the threatening e-mails. Unfortunately, there was not enough evidence available to make an arrest. Once the police got involved, the e-mails ceased, which led me to believe that at least one of the people questioned, including Franklin, was indeed the culprit.

By the time Franklin was in jail and I was going through the divorce, my co-workers and friends began to question my weight loss and my appearance in general. I became so thin that even I became alarmed. My body felt like I was carrying a mountain on my shoulders. I walked Kane, my German shepherd, every morning before going to work and twice in the evening — immediately when I arrived home from work and just before going to bed. I began to fall often while walking him, and for no apparent reason, but I dismissed it as my being "clumsy." I was tired all the time, irritable and achy, and barely able to get out of bed in the mornings, but I forced myself to walk Kane. He sensed something was wrong as well. When we were out walking, he sensed when to slow down, look up at me, and at times just stop. I loved my dog, and when you saw me, you saw Kane. I didn't know then how sick I was, but I knew something was wrong and attributed it my stressful life. My balance was awful, but I shrugged it off as a sinus disorder and allergies.

It was not long until it got to the point where I did not have enough energy to take care of Kane. With the help of a pet adoption agency, referred through the luxury dog spa where Kane occasionally spent time,

Franklin Returns to his Roots

we found my best friend a loving home. I was struggling with my health and caring for the dog had become too much for me physically and financially. I still miss Kane and to this day, whenever I see a German Shepherd, my eyes fill with tears. It helps me to know that he is with a loving couple. I am told that he has an older brother, a Rottweiler, and that the owner brings both of the dogs to the spa for monthly grooming. I smile when I hear that because Kane became accustomed to the good life. I am better now because I know he is loved, but I will always remember him and miss him. My friends often ask if I will get another German Shepherd and I reply, "I really would like to, but there can never be another Kane. Also, my health does not permit me to take on the many responsibilities of caring for a dog."

CHAPTER 33
A SURPISE OVERNIGHT DELIVERY

In September 2007, I received an overnight express package marked URGENT from a title company in Pennsylvania regarding a recent refinance of the property that my mother left my brother Toby, and me. Thrift, her husband, had a life tenancy in the home. The letter requested that I sign a document from the refinancing of the home that was executed by Thrift that I knew absolutely nothing about. The letter indicated that because I was a remainderman to my mother's estate, it was necessary that I sign the loan papers because I was not present at settlement, which I knew absolutely nothing about. The property was refinanced for $165,000, leaving my one-half interest in the home totally usurped. Of course, I did not sign the papers and immediately sought legal counsel regarding yet another nightmare added to the existing ones. More anxiety and more legal fees. My brother coerced my stepfather into refinancing the house as a life tenant. The problem with this is that by law he was not authorized to refinance or encumber the property without my signature.

Beginning in 2005, before the illegal refinance occurred, I asked Thrift to probate my mother's property because, at that time, she had been deceased seven years and she named him as personal representative. He refused to probate the property as required, because Ma left a Last Will and Testament, which had been filed in probate court. My brother couldn't care less about anything but making babies across the DC metropolitan area.

Because Thrift would not probate my mother's property as required by law, I attempted to get an appointment from the court to take care of the matter. My brother and stepfather were uncooperative and because of the mounting legal fees and their total lack of cooperation, I was forced to abandon the matter at least for the time being.

Two years later, in April 2007, my brother told me that he retained an attorney to probate the property bequeathed to us by our mother. According to him, the attorney was charging him only $500 when I had incurred legal fees in excess of $2,000 in an attempt to probate the property. He was so determined to have me sign the probate documents that he came to my home and personally drove me downtown to his attorney's office. I signed the documents, satisfied to know that we finally got the business of my mother's estate taken care of. I should have known he was up to something. It's not like him to be decent or fair about anything. I should have suspected something, but I wrongly thought that after seven years since our mother's death, he perhaps had gotten a grip on the importance of probating the property. I wanted to believe that he figured out the importance of having the property in our names and not in the name of our deceased mother. I explained to him numerous times the tax and other benefits of having the home deeded to us, not to mention the fact that Thrift had moved out of the home years earlier.

Because Toby did not pay child support for most of his fourteen children, the State of Maryland suspended his commercial driver's license and that was the reason that he and Thrift went behind my back and took all the equity out of the property. In addition, a final accounting was required by the personal representative to close the probate case. All beneficiaries listed in the will must be notified of any pending activity regarding the property. When I received a copy of the final accounting, I sent a letter to the judge opposing it, because it did not list the $165,000 taken from the property without my consent and the matter was in litigation.

Thrift died of cancer on the day Barack Obama was sworn into office as the president of the United States. I had no knowledge that he was ill. As a matter of fact, my brother did not want me to know about his illness or his death, much less attend the funeral. Two weeks after Thrift's funeral, Toby went to see my son to ask him to check with me to see if I

A Surprise Overnight Delivery

would consider family counseling. I could not believe that he had the gall to ask about family counseling. Now that the only person who would help him with his evil deeds was gone, he wanted family counseling. I was now extremely cognizant of the characteristics of demons. Like Beyoncé's song said, "He must not know 'bout me!" Now that my mother and Thrift were deceased, Toby had no one at his beck and call and it was certainly not going to be me.

After leaving a business meeting one morning, I entered my office to check my phone voice mail as I always do and there was a message from my brother, "Hey Nesa, this yo' brotha. Give me a call." As far as I was concerned, I didn't have a brother, not even a half-brother. I did not return the call, and was furious that he would have the audacity to call me except to refund the money that he and Thrift stole from me. Because I was listed as joint owner on the property, the bank was coming after both of us in an attempt to put a lien on the property. I found it interesting that the bank was now keenly aware of my status for the purpose of repaying the loan, but somehow made the mistake of overlooking my ownership when executing an illegal loan. In June 2009, we had to appear before a judge to schedule a date for a hearing. We appeared at a mediation session regarding the property with a mediator, two attorneys from Chase Bank, and my attorney. Toby was unimaginably vulgar and insulting to me and my attorney. He boldly stated to me during the mediation that "if you dropped dead right now I wouldn't bother to pick you up." I was already hurt but his pronouncement almost knocked me off my feet. Even after that incident, I tried to work with him briefly to get the house ready for sale, but it didn't work out — he's just too evil. God said to forgive 7x7, but he did not say that your enemies had to be in your space.

CHAPTER 34

TIME TO HEAL

Depressed and distraught, in February 2007, I began therapy with Dr. Gregory Wheeler. We discussed my failed marriage, Franklin's incarceration, and the blame placed on me by him for his troubles, as well as the extreme verbal, emotional, and mental abuse that I suffered. I remained in therapy with Dr. Wheeler for one year. The sessions focused on my depression and ways to help me make sound decisions concerning my impending divorce and my life. My failed marriage and divorce-in-progress were beginning to take a serious psychological and emotional toll on me. A short time before our sessions ended, Dr. Wheeler encouraged me to continue in therapy to address my generalized anxiety disorder and depression.

In November 2008, I applied for admittance to group counseling sessions with a Family Crisis Center in Maryland. I was evaluated and assessed, and it was determined that I was a victim of emotional, verbal, and mental abuse by Franklin Carter. To be accepted into the center, I had to commit to a 12-week program. At first, I was hesitant to participate, believing I did not have sufficient time to devote to the program, given my work schedule. However, there was no doubt in my mind that I needed help to move forward with my life and I committed myself to the program. I was assigned to a victims' support group, where I met women who had or were having similar experiences.

This proved to be the best intervention I could ever have. The group leader showed empathy and was sympathetic to all of us, but was straight to the point about domestic abuse and its cycle of violence. She stressed to the group that it was up to us to change our lives. The one thing that she emphasized to the group was, "It's not your fault that you loved your partner, and you will love again." That's the part I could not fathom.

Under the expert leadership of our group leader and strong group support, I began to get a handle on my anger. I made a decision to become motivated again by finding a way to finish what I started — to fight for the Ph.D., to continue where I left off somehow. I earnestly wanted to participate in the group process to learn about domestic abuse, and to heal so that I could accept the fact that I was not to blame for any of the abuse that I encountered, nor was I to blame for making decisions to leave hostile and dangerous relationships. At my halfway point in the program, my counselor told me that when I first joined the group, I displayed extreme anger. As a direct result of the trauma that I experienced throughout most of my life, I had become angry and bitter. My group leader worked diligently with me to help me to let go of the anger so I could move forward. I am so thankful to the crisis center for its support.

CHAPTER 35

MULTIPLE SCLEROSIS

F or some unknown reason, I was steadily losing weight. At first, I
was so overwhelmed by my life challenges that I did not notice
the severity of the weight loss, although I was questioned often
about my health by friends and co-workers. I finally went to the doctor
for a check-up and as he asked me general health questions, I told him
about my imbalance and frequent falls. He asked more questions about
the falls I experienced, but I shrugged it off as simply being clumsy. He
began to focus on my imbalance and falls and recommended that I get a
brain MRI. I was shocked at his suggestion, and asked why. "I'm just
clumsy," I said. I went on to tell him about the divorce and the extreme
stress I was experiencing. He insisted on the brain MRI, and I reluctantly
agreed. I truly believed the weight loss was due to anxiety and stress and
all I needed to do was to get through the divorce and I would be good as
new.

Less than a week after taking the brain MRI, I received a telephone
call from my doctor. We talked in general for a while about how I was
feeling. He paused and told me that he received the results of the brain
MRI and that it was abnormal. I asked what that meant. He told me that
the radiologist who reviewed the test results indicated that the abnormal-
ity could be a result of high blood pressure, diabetes, AIDS, or any number of other disorders. He made arrangements for me to see a well-known
neurologist as soon as possible.

I first saw a neurologist at Washington Hospital Center, who reviewed
the MRI and told me that he strongly suspected I had multiple sclerosis.

He encouraged me to make an appointment at Georgetown University Hospital because of its excellent MS facility and specialists. I made an appointment at Georgetown and met with a top neurologist, who had spent ten years at the National Institutes of Health rescarching multiple sclerosis. At first, I was unsure about this new doctor, but when I met him, I was immediately comfortable. Dr. Manuel Gutierrez, from South America, was a pleasant, gentle, heavyset man with a thick Spanish accent. He took considerable time with me and it became obvious that accurately diagnosing my medical condition was important to him. There was a calm energy about him that transferred to me. I was more than frightened, but the turning point was when he told me that whatever my illness turned out to be, we would work it out together. I learned to trust him and had no doubt that he was competent in the field of neurology and a specialist in multiple sclerosis. More importantly, he would be straight with me about my illness and I believed he would take care of me as best he could. Before he would diagnose me with multiple sclerosis, he was determined to rule out other possible diseases explaining that my symptoms mimicked a number of disorders, including Lyme disease.

When I went back to see him for what I thought would be his diagnosis, he decided it was necessary to do another battery of tests. One thing I was confident about was that my doctor was extremely thorough, checking for everything that could tell us what was wrong with me. He wanted to be absolutely sure about the diagnosis.

After the second battery of tests did not give him the information he was looking for, he had no choice but to schedule a spinal tap. He was hoping that it would not come to a spinal tap but this test would tell him for certain whether I had MS.

The spinal tap confirmed that I definitely had multiple sclerosis. At this point, I was pencil-thin because I was still highly stressed and ill with multiple sclerosis. Through it all, I remained calm, taking in every bit of information and listening to treatment options to slow the progression of the disease. I already had strong faith in God so there was no need to worry because I knew he would not put more on me than I could bear. That's what God promised, and that's where I put my faith.

Dr. Gutierrez and I decided that I needed time to think seriously about the treatment options because with MS, once the treatment is started, it is for life — there is no turning back. MS is a progressive neurological disease that affects the brain and the spinal cord. It is a disease that affects movement, and in severe cases causes paralysis, blindness, and possibly death. For seventeen years, I was diagnosed with fibromyalgia but it is very possible that it was MS all the while. I found out that fibromyalgia can occur with MS, which is difficult to diagnose because it mimics so many other diseases as well.

After receiving the final diagnosis, I went home and prayed, asking God to take care of me and to help me make a decision about my treatment plan. His familiar soft voice reassured me that I would be victorious in this battle and to hold onto my faith. He has never forsaken me or left me, and He never will.

The day that was set aside for me to decide on a treatment plan arrived. Dr. Gutierrez and I agreed on daily, subcutaneous injections of Copaxone, rather than an MS medication that requires more painful weekly injections into a muscle, with flu-like side effects. Copaxone is a brand of Glatiramer acetate, which is in a class of drugs called immunomodulators that work by stopping the body from damaging its own nerve cells.

Medication for MS is unbelievably expensive. Initially, my medication cost $3,200 per month for 30 syringes. Thankfully in 2011, a change in Copaxone suppliers lowered the cost to $3,200 for 90 syringes. Use of this medication enables me to continue with my life uninterrupted. I have learned to live with MS with an unwavering faith in God and with the support of my son, friends, doctor, my MS nurse — who calls me like clock-work once a month to check on me — and an MS support organization. When I am tired, I rest. When my body is sore, I swim because it is soothing, or I get a massage that directs energy throughout my body. When situations or circumstances stress me, I seek God, prayer, and quiet. I am careful about my circle of friends, and am careful not to get caught up in other folks' mess.

CHAPTER 36
FREE AT LAST

In December 2007, Franklin was still incarcerated and the date for the divorce hearing was close. Franklin had given Regina, his oldest sister, power of attorney to take care of his legal business and to act in his stead throughout the divorce ordeal. My attorney, Alan Steinbert, a middle-aged Jewish man, represented my interests and a young African American lawyer, Monica Stevens, represented Franklin and began the hearing by informing the judge that her client was absent because he was incarcerated. When the judge, a white woman who looked to be in her early forties, asked why he was incarcerated, his attorney stated, "Because of a restraining order that his wife took out." The judge looked perplexed and asked when the protection order was taken out. She replied, "In December 2006." The judge became visibly angry and told her that the reason given was impossible because a person can only be held for sixty days on a protection order. She asked Franklin's attorney again why he was incarcerated. My counsel quickly stepped up and answered, "Your honor, he is in jail on a gun charge that revoked his parole." The explanation was reasonable to the judge. Ms. Stevens obviously had not done her homework, or relied solely on what her client, a pathological liar, told her.

Franklin was scheming to stall the divorce because he was hoping he could get released before the divorce was granted. His attorney advocated for a continued legal separation until her client was released from prison. She indicated to the judge that the property settlement would be finalized upon his release. He was due to be released in June 2008. My attorney argued that I met the required waiting period and should be granted a divorce without further delay. The judge told my attorney that she did not have the authority to grant a divorce hearing based on Franklin's motion, but she recommended that he meet with the chief judge, who was in her chambers. My heart felt like it had stopped. Both attorneys marched quickly to see the chief judge, and thankfully, she was in her chambers and agreed to see them. I was not allowed inside the judge's chambers so my witness, Egypt C. L. Dawson, and I sat outside in the hall praying that she would grant a divorce hearing before Franklin was released from prison. My attorney emerged from the judge's chamber with Franklin's attorney and told me that the judge granted the divorce hearing, scheduled for February 2008. I was ecstatic! I could see the light at the end of the tunnel. Free at last, free at last, thank God Almighty, I'm going to be free at last!

In preparation for the divorce hearing, the house was appraised and financial disclosures and other information were provided as required. Franklin wanted the house to be sold, even though the mortgage was "upside down." Because of the housing crash and recession, more was owed on the house than its value. He wanted to do anything to keep me from living in my home. When he realized that was not going to happen, he asked for $50,000 out of my 401K plan, the majority of the furniture, even knick-knacks on the tables and pictures off the wall hoping to leave me with an empty house.

When my lawyer presented me with Franklin's demands, I gave a hearty laugh. It was quite hilarious! This fool came into the marriage with nothing. Nada. When I left Derrick Frye, I vowed that no man would cause me to lose what I worked for ever again, and I meant it. Because of the recent equitable-distribution law in Maryland, spouses were able to keep pretty much what they brought into the marriage as long as it could be proven. My attorney understood that I was not giving Franklin any more than I absolutely had to and he knew not to present me with foolishness about what Franklin Carter wanted.

Egypt and Helen, two close girlfriends, went to court with me. The judge, a white, middle-aged, no-nonsense woman, read the settlement agreement: I would keep the house that I built and Franklin was to sign the deed over to me. I would pay off his $10,000 line of credit, and give him $10,000 from my 401K plan. He would also get a bedroom set, pool table, red lamp, red picture, one of two wall water fountains, fax machine, laptop computer, his car, clothes, and other personal items. The judge looked at me and asked if I was satisfied with the settlement. I responded that I was. She looked at me and asked, "Are you sure?" I replied, "Yes, your honor, I am sure." When the judge was satisfied that the agreement was in order, she looked at me and said, "Congratulations." Franklin's attorney stated to the judge that additional time was needed because she had to get the documents to her client, who was incarcerated in North Carolina. The judge looked up at her and curtly told her that it was not necessary to send the papers to her client, that she as the judge had the authority to sign off on the divorce document. The judge told both counselors to get the papers to her for signature and that was that! Her attitude and demeanor demonstrated that she intended to get me divorced from that loser! I believe she knew that I had been through enough!

Franklin was released in March 2008 with a permanent no-contact condition of parole regarding me. It was not surprising that he refused to sign the deed to the house over to me as ordered by the court. Almost a year later, I took him back to court for refusing to sign the deed that would end all of our business together. Actually, that's all he was waiting for because he knew the day would come when I would take action to remove him from the deed. I retained new counsel, Lynda Gandy, an African American attorney, to handle this matter. Because of a conflict on her calendar, her partner, an ex-police commander, represented me at the hearing. A sheriff was requested to be present in the courtroom because of the permanent no-contact condition issued by the United States Parole Commission to ensure my safety. Of course, Franklin came to court *pro se*. In his warped mind, there is absolutely no one smarter than him; therefore no one was better able to represent him than himself. He had his imbecile protégé cousin with him again to provide false testimony as usual. Franklin had the audacity to come to court with bloodshot eyes, probably from drinking, smoking reefer, or both, on the way to court.

During the court session regarding the deed, Franklin attempted to bring trumped-up charges against me for supposedly damaging his car that was housed in my garage for the eighteen months that he was in prison and for not returning everything that belonged to him as stipulated in the divorce settlement agreement, including a woman's gold ring. The judge, a large white man with a stern demeanor, was patient with him in the beginning, but over time became annoyed with Franklin. The judge explained that we were there on the issue of the deed. He explained to Franklin that if he had a complaint about property not being turned over as agreed upon, he would have to file the correct motion and get a hearing date set. The session continued regarding the deed. Franklin was acting so ignorant that the judge had to tell him to shut up on a few occasions when I asked for permission to address the court. The judge was clearly annoyed and asked him point blank, "Are you going to sign the dumb thing or not?" Franklin replied, "I'm not signing anything until I get what is due me." The judge leaned back in his chair, looked at him, and said, "You either sign the deed today or I will assign a trustee." He asked my attorney who would be the trustee and she answered that she would serve in that capacity. The judge then turned to Franklin and sternly asked, "What do you want to do?" Big bad Franklin backed down and said, "I'll sign it."

The deed was signed within minutes and my attorney promptly notarized it. That was one happy day. I returned home with renewed vigor. Bright and early the following morning, I visited the Recorder of Deeds in Prince George's County and within thirty minutes my house became solely mine. It was now legally my home and I was the sole owner.

In January 2009, Franklin and I were in court again. As before, a sheriff was required to be present to enforce the permanent no-contact order and to ensure my safety. This time, he was suing me for $4,200 for alleged damages to his 2000 Lincoln Continental and items that he claimed I did not turn over to him. The items that he alleged were not returned included his passport, which I found in my private lockbox, and provided to him during the hearing. His enabler sister, Regina, falsely testifed that when the car was retrieved from my garage, it did not have a battery in it. I was rather shocked that she would lower herself to his level by telling such an untruth and under oath, even though she worked for a law firm. His car, which sat in my garage accumulating dirt, dust, and flat tires, had not been started in over a year; the battery was dead, but clearly it had not been removed. I looked at her and shook my head. I felt pity for her. She looked old, worried, and worn out. Her brother was doing to her what he does to everybody who allows it. His goal is to control and conquer when it serves his interest and to hell with the consequences for anybody other than himself.

This hearing was quite the circus. Franklin thought he was Perry Mason while examining his sister and nephew on the witness stand. After he questioned his two witnesses, the judge asked my attorney to call her witnesses. Ms. Gandy confidently stood up and respectfully told the judge that Mr. Carter had proved nothing and that she was calling for the judge's decision. Franklin's plan backfired again. He was waiting to get me on the witness stand for cross-examination. That would be his only opportunity to address me without going back to jail because of the permanent no-contact order. I saw to that! As a result of my attorney's action, he would not get his chance to say anything to me. The judge ruled in my favor — that as far as the law was concerned, the agreement had been met and the agreed upon items were returned, except for the woman's gold ring that to this day I never found. The judge stated, "If there was a problem with the transfer of the property, it should have been brought to the court's attention then, not a year later." The judge's words were music to my ears when he announced that the case was closed. God brought me through yet again!

Before leaving court, Franklin and I were required to sign a court document. The bailiff gave Franklin his copy to sign and then gave a copy to me. Franklin and I were positioned on opposite sides of the courtroom. He signed the court document and instead of waiting for the bailiff to retrieve his signed document, he walked across the courtroom to where I was sitting and stood close enough to practically touch my leg.

Upon leaving the court, flanked by my son and attorney, I walked by the man who was now legally and completely out of my life. I triumphantly walked down the hall, pressure lifted, my body swaying with my head held high and my shoulders squared. It was over. Thank you, God, we won! I knew with all certainty that if it were not for my strong relationship with God, I would have lost my mind.

AGAINST ALL ODDS

I successfully passed the doctoral political science and public administration comprehensive examinations in January 2008. In December 2009, I successfully defended my dissertation proposal, and in July 2010, I completed all requirements for the doctor of philosophy degree. I graduated from Howard University on May 14, 2011, with a Ph.D. in black politics, public administration, and education administration. My dissertation examines the disparate mandatory minimum sentences that directly and/or indirectly target poor, uneducated African American women, usually for possession of small amounts of crack cocaine that removes them from their families and communities. These draconian laws resulted in the imprisonment of thousands of non-violent women of color who spent years in prison because of unfair and unjust laws.

LESSONS LEARNED

Faith in God, writing this book, therapy, and participation in a domestic violence program have helped me to recover. Here are a few of the lessons that I have learned.

1. God comes first!

2. My abuse stemmed from family dysfunction. My father was emotionally and physically abusive to the women in his life, and my mother was abused by her first husband. Other women in my family were also abused by their husbands and partners. I learned as a child that abuse was "normal."

3. I repeatedly became involved in abusive relationships because I was not taught about the qualities to look for in a man. I didn't know better, so I could not choose better.

4. Abusers don't change without intervention.

5. If a man was not in my life, I felt something was lacking. I accepted the wrong men in my life to avoid loneliness. I am now learning to enjoy being in my own space by myself. At times, being alone is still a struggle, but one that I embrace.

6. Once I got in touch with a higher power and began to rely on spiritual strength, and placed my faith in God, I became stronger and wiser.

7. "Sista" support is important. Women and girls need each other to survive in good and bad times.

8. Parents must teach their sons and daughters that abuse and violence is wrong. They must teach both genders to love and respect each other as individuals.

Hallelujah Happy

There were times in my life when I believed that I would never be happy. It seemed to me that everything I tried to do back-fired in my face. I unconsciously placed men before God, and as a matter of fact, did not even think to seek His counsel. Now, I can shout that I am hallelujah happy. I have figured out who I am and what I am not; what I will tolerate and what I will not. I am a spiritual woman who places God before anything and anybody. I seek His counsel for everything to the point that sometimes I think that I must get on His last nerve.

I am hallelujah happy because God walked me through the fire. I was burned by the flames but I was not disfigured. He allowed me to keep my sanity when I could have easily lost my mind. He did not allow multiple sclerosis to knock me off my feet, but used it instead to show His mercy and give me a testimony. I can still walk, swim, and dance. I walk to witness God's magnificent work, I dance to praise God, and I dance because I'm free. I dance because I am happy and I dance because I can. I swim because that's when I talk to God, listen for his counsel, and make decisions.

I am hallelujah happy because he kept me in my home when I could barely pay the mortgage. I am hallelujah happy because God gave favor to allow me to become a scholar amongst the chaos. He moved mountains that were in my way so that I would reach my goal to receive a Ph.D.

I am hallelujah happy because my son and granddaughter are healthy and thriving and for the love and encouragement of a few friends who have journeyed with me through my trials and tribulations. I am hallelujah happy because of His gift of resiliency that helped me to battle my demons and become victorious.

Finally, I am hallelujah happy because I personally know about the miracles of God — the battles that were fought and won simply by being obedient to His word. "No hand raised against me shall prosper (Isaiah 54:17)," was the spiritual foundation of my triumph and I urge you to find yours. Love should not hurt; rather, love heals.

I am HALLELUJAH HAPPY because STILL I STAND, and so can you!

.

CPSIA information can be obtained at www.ICGtesting.com
Printed in the USA
LVOW13s2346140414

381680LV00001B/5/P

9 781457 506567